Transpersonal Dynamics

Transpersonal Dynamics

The Relational Field, Depth Work
and the Unconscious

Stacey Millichamp

MA (Psych) UKCP

TransPersonal
Press

TransPersonal Press
(*a Kaminn Media imprint*)
Delft Cottage, Dyke
Forres IV36 2TF
Scotland
transpersonalpress.com

A CIP record for this title is available from the British Library.

ISBN 978-1-912698-00-4 (print)
ISBN 978-1-912698-01-1 (ebook)

Cover illustrations by Dan Hillier (danhillier.com)
Edited by Kathleen White (intheworkscoaching.com)
Text design and layout by Thierry Bogliolo

Printed, bound and distributed by Ingram Spark

Contents

List of Illustrations

Introduction

My years as a trainer with psychotherapy and supervision students have taught me that teaching material shifts and changes in unexpected and unusual ways according to the particular training group sitting in front of me. This means that I have to hold my agenda in an open hand, with a willingness to allow the particular dynamic and field conditions of this group of people to emerge and co-create the material that I will deliver. Each moment and each group present different requirements, despite my carefully planned curriculum. This way of working requires courage and a capacity to operate in the unknown, rather than clinging to familiar ground, which as a trainer is a challenge, given the potential for public criticism. Yet time and again, I have experienced groups coming alive and experiencing catalytic change when risk taking allows us all to leap into the current moment.

I have long felt that the psychotherapy world has come to place too much emphasis on creating supportive safety for clients, which usually means practitioners being relatively quiet and not intruding too much on the client's space, emphasizing support rather than challenge and keeping spontaneity to a minimum. Authentic responses are traditionally taken to clinical supervision, where the therapist's countertransference is decoded with the supervisor, sanitized and taken back to the client as 'their stuff', rather than engaging with the relational dynamics to create alive, charged possibilities that therapist and client can explore together. This leads to an undemocratic dynamic where clients are taking all the risks, and therapists are sitting in a tightly controlled state of confluence, never disturbing the client for fear of generating too much unpredictable conflict or intimacy.

Intimacy requires an equal amount of risk taking and authenticity as together client and therapist find their way through to what is occurring in the here and now. Most therapy trainings teach therapists to be reflectively controlled through cultivating the appearance of a neutral expert, rather than the development of an immanent relationship. Clients often sense that their therapist is withholding important information, and if they have the courage to say this they are asked to examine their fantasy as a projection, to assess the purpose of their question, or to address potential resistance to being open and honest, rather than the therapist addressing their own fear of being more authentic.

I see therapists burning out or getting sick and dropping out of their work as a result of the inauthentic amount of control that they are exerting in the therapeutic space. It is perhaps time for psychotherapy and counselling to find ways of engaging with the here and now in a more dynamic way, one that allows clients the respect of a more authentic relationship and therapists a more honest, mutually explorative way forward.

The experience I have often had of the current here and now of a group or a client, evoking responses that move me as a teacher and therapist beyond my role as benevolent practitioner, reminds me of a curious dream that sparked off the origins of this book. In the dream I was being shown a metaphor for the relatedness of life by Dr Arnold Mindell, a physicist and psychotherapist who is the founder of process work; he pointed at the body of a man whose component parts (organs, limbs) separated and took on whole bodies of their own, yet stayed connected to the main body via waves which I saw as lines of connectedness. He expressed that the whole (original) body needed these parts to individuate and explore life and reality as fully as possible, to discover their own particular natures, and that this experience radiated back to the whole body as information that expanded and evolved that body.

In this way, the parts represented various ways in which the whole body could explore itself as completely as possible, using that experience and information to expand and develop, simply for the purpose that to explore and experience is a pleasurable, creative and joyful act. The message seemed to be that the original body represented the 'whole' from which we come and that we, and all of life around us, were the parts on personal, yet universal journeys – couriers of precious information that create universal evolution as we fully define and experience our uniqueness.

This description of the creative act that we might all be a part of seems to fit descriptions of the Tao:

The Tao
> *pours out everything into life –*
It is a cornucopia
> *that never runs dry.*

It is the deep source of everything –
> *it is nothing, and yet in everything.*

It smooths round sharpness
and untangles the knots.

It glows like the lamp
that draws the moth...

Tao exists, Tao is
but where It came from I do not know.

It has been shaping things
> *from before the First Being,*
> *from before the Beginning of Time.*[1]

This idea of a fluid, creative Self leads us into consideration of how we are viewing the creative flux and flow of a therapy session. That beyond our skills to work intrapsychically or interpersonally, there may be a particular type of interest that we can cultivate towards the subtle unfolding of what is present and emerging; that if we are indeed connected to a Universal Self, then surely, we must be sharing a 'field' with our clients into which and from which Self is incarnating? We could begin to take an interest in what would change in the therapy room if we viewed each session as a time in which we bring awareness to being inexorably linked to an emerging process that creatively arises out of the coming together of two people with an intention to focus on 'what is occurring'.

This is not necessarily a big change for practitioners who have a solid grounding in the use of transference and countertransference, in which it is assumed that the therapist's experience is information about the client's process (as well as indicators of where the therapist might be getting stimulated with their own unconscious material). However, this subtle shift of attitude seems to have a big effect on us as therapists and on the experience of our clients: generating a sense of emerging mystery, a feeling of creativity without having to 'do anything' creative, an experience of greater democracy within the therapeutic relationship, and a sense of connectedness.

This book has its origins in these experiences and, after many years as a trainer, the content explored in the following chapters has arisen out of the material that students and qualified therapists have found most useful. These ideas focus on concepts from physics that give us alternatives for assessing 'reality' and some ideas from 'Universalist' approaches that are emerging in spiritual and ecological forms in the West, drawing on ways of working with the transferential phenomena that bring in interrelated approaches. I have developed these contextual influences into methids for mapping the meaning encoded within the landscape of client work, utilizing ordinary language rather than clinical language. Language is an important tool for therapists, and we need to support the development of an everyday vocabulary that is immediately usable for practitioners from all theoretical approaches, rather than supporting semantic separation.

I hope this book inspires you towards a more relational approach that is dynamic, immediate and meaningful.

—*Stacey Millichamp, May 2018*

---

[1] M. Kwok, M. Palmer, and J. Ramsey (trans), *Tao Te Ching* (USA, Australia, Great Britain: Elements Books Ltd., 1993), p. 32.

Chapter 1

The Context of Psychosynthesis: past and present

Any school of thought that develops does so within a field of influence that is permeated by the socio-economic, scientific, educational and political themes of its day. As a starting point to this book's inquiry into new ways of working with psychosynthesis models, it is important to look at the historical context in which Assagioli conducted his research into and development of psychosynthesis theory and to begin to assess how today's changing scientific and social climate might impact our theories of the Self.

Assagioli: life and influences

Assagioli trained as a medical student in Florence in 1906, where he lived most of his life. He subsequently trained as an analyst and psychiatrist, during which time he developed the concepts and theory of psychosynthesis. At the beginning of the 20th century there was an upwelling of exciting ideas in all areas of thought. Influences from the East were beginning to come into the West and therefore religious thought was being re-examined. At the same time, education was being revolutionized by such thinkers as Montessori, Froebel and Steiner, and the unconscious was being scientifically studied by Freud, among others.

This was therefore very much of a Renaissance time and accordingly Assagioli drew from many fields and influences. Inherent in the development of his ideas are both a scientific and a mystical approach, though he tended to play down the more mystical aspects of his work, intent on gaining scientific validity for his theories. His background training in medicine and psychiatry also included psychoanalysis and thus there are strong psychodynamic roots in psychosynthesis. In his doctoral thesis Assagioli gave a critique of Freud's approach, claiming it was incomplete, as it did not address the actualized elements of human nature or how to enable man to fully live his potential. From early on he challenged the purely scientific and reductionist attitudes of the time, bringing to the forefront the possibility that man also has self-actualizing potential which can be stimulated and developed.

Assagioli was influenced by many spiritual and philosophical traditions and people, such as the Russian esotericist P. D. Ouspensky, the Sufi mystic Inayat Khan Rehmat Khan Pathan, Carl Jung, Martin Buber – who developed the I-Thou relationship theory, the founder of Logotherapy Viktor Frankl, and Alice Bailey, with whom he was a close friend. His concerns were focussed on the healing of psychological fragmentation and the possibility for synthesis at both an individual and collective level, including an interest in education and social issues. These spiritual and mystical influences mean that within psychosynthesis lies a deeply optimistic and structured approach, not just to personal development but also to spiritual synthesis, individually and culturally, in which the person is able to find a meaningful, purposeful and interconnected place within the whole.

Wider contexts and paradigms

If we look at the wider political and scientific context of Assagioli's life (and indeed for much of the 20th century), we begin to see that there was (and still is) inherent in the culture a split between religion and science and, more deeply, a 'myth of isolation' infusing the West during this time.[1] Therefore, despite the exciting movements and potential of the early 20th century, there may have been tendencies towards implicit beliefs of separateness, not just within the development of psychosynthesis but also in the way it is practised now. I make this assertion because there is much evidence to suggest that the culture and its prevailing scientific paradigm has a very powerful impact on us as individuals whether we overtly 'agree' with it or not. It becomes part of our psyche, something that is especially obvious in how we address the ways we are connected to the collective unconscious, which is explored in detail in the following chapters.

Jean Hardy cites Thomas Kuhn's work, *The Structure of Scientific Revolutions*, in which he states that there is a predominant scientific paradigm at any one time which creates a set of models about the nature of the world. This opinion is echoed by Hardy again in her pamphlet *There is Another World, but it is This One*, in which she expresses Karl Mannheim's view that 'the main institutions in that society... will represent that dominant set of assumptions about the nature of the society and its picture of reality'.[2] These predominant paradigms affect our innermost being, influencing the way in which we construct reality and make meaning of the world around us.

The living cosmos gives way to the clockwork universe

In her book *Quantum Self*, Donar Zohar states that in this century we have been plagued by an alienation between consciousness and matter, a sense that we are strangers in this world. She traces the roots of this alienation back to Plato's distinction between the realm of ideas and experience, through Christianity's favouring of the soul over the body (or at the cost of the body as somehow a vessel for sin), and into the 17th century philosophical and scientific revolution which brought in Cartesian doubt and Newtonian physics. The living cosmos of Greek and mediaeval times – in which the universe is filled with mystery, intelligence and purpose – was replaced by the conception of the universe as a clockwork machine.

The paradigm that emerged from the scientific, economic and industrial revolutions of the 17th and 18th centuries was therefore one which viewed the world as predetermined and potentially predictable, in which the whole can be objectively understood by examining the parts. Life is made up of isolated, independent objects. As human beings we are therefore rooted in nothing bigger than ourselves. Descartes' theories added to this sense of separateness by splitting the mind off from the body, claiming that mind and matter are essentially separate and that we must therefore set out with the objective power of our minds to control nature (our own and that around us). This paradigm, with its 'myth' of rational thinking, claims that the only worthwhile knowledge or truth is that which is quantifiable and can be empirically proven. Darwin and Marx, with their theories of evolution, compounded this myth in the later part of their lives, leaving us with a sense that there is no wonder in life, that only the material world really exists, which evolves through biological processes. The soul was gone from the body, replaced by a transcendental vision in which good/God is seen as coming down to matter from a long way up and to which a soul must travel a long journey before coming 'home' again.

The interconnected cosmos

It was not until the 1960s that this prevailing paradigm was truly questioned with an emerging sense that we are interconnected with each other and life and that we thus need to take responsibility for ourselves and the world around us. Along with this social force for change, science was consolidating new visions of reality which had been worked on since the turn of the century. In his book *Quantum Theology*, Diarmuid O'Murchu cites the philosopher-scientist Arthur Koestler who suggested that we call each whole thing within nature (previously viewed as separate parts) a 'holon'. A holon is a whole made up of its own parts, whilst also being part of a larger whole. It must both preserve its own autonomy and function as part of the larger whole in order to survive. No creature or system can be entirely independent, as each system (holon) is part of a larger system (holon) into which it must integrate in order to survive. As well as being a word that describes interdependence, it is an emerging cultural image that takes us beyond the mechanistic metaphor.

It was in the 1960s, amidst such radical changes in society, that Assagioli's teachings began to be more internationally accepted. His theory of psychosynthesis created a way of working with fragmented parts to enable an eventual synthesis and potential wholeness. He saw this as applicable on many levels, from the individual through to the global collective. Here we come to definitions of the Self that include both transcendent and immanent visions of a spiritual sphere.

The Self

Let's explore these ideas briefly and begin to assess how, if at all, there may be a tendency for Newtonian mechanistic thinking (and therefore splitting soul and matter) within psychosynthesis theory and practice.

Assagioli describes the Self as follows: 'This Self is above, and unaffected by, the flow of the mind-stream or by bodily conditions; and the personal conscious self should be considered merely as its reflection, it's "projection" in the field of the personality'.[3] Diana Whitmore describes the Self as 'the point of pure, essential being which is unaffected by conscious experience... the Experiencer... the Self is a field of energy containing phenomena of a superconscious nature, and providing the conditions for evolution, development and growth... the Self is unchanging in its essence...'.[4]

Whitmore points out the difference between the Self and the Superconscious. The former is pure Being and contentless, sending energies that are transmitted through the Superconscious making them available to the personality (should the personality choose to embrace them). The Superconscious has many experiences and content within it, whereas direct experience of the Self is usually attained once one is able to dis-identify from unconscious and superconscious content.

The 'I' in psychosynthesis theory is seen as the outpost of the Self, the point of conscious awareness that receives impulses from the Self and assimilates them from moment to moment. The process of therapy is one in which personal synthesis is initially approached by working through some of the archaic elements within the lower unconscious, often followed by an existential crisis and re-evaluation, finally exploring the transpersonal realm with a personality integrated enough to make use of the superconscious influences and effects.

Given some of the changing scientific and philosophical paradigms, we could begin to ask:

- Whether the Self is indeed unchanging and contentless. Many contemporary physicists (e.g., Baeyer and Zohar) are suggesting that what we previously took to be empty spaces in the universe are actually 'full' with quantum potential from which new impulses are constantly being born and which seem to consist of blueprints which govern patterns for the future. This might indicate that Self belongs to or is a part of a great web of potential, from which things are created and to which these experiences and relational interactions flow back. In other words, that there is an evolutionary process occurring that includes the Self.

- Whether the Universal Self is made manifest most purely in the relational elements within therapy. Quantum physicists are assessing the apparent reality that we are as individuals determined by the quality of our interdependence on others, in other words, that we are our relationships (in the broadest sense). We will be looking at this concept in greater depth in the next chapter, but at this point it is worth raising the question of whether the Self is individual at all, but rather is the point at which the personality makes contact with the creative process of life itself.

These questions are raised with the intention of exploring more deeply our own unconscious attitudes that may be attached to an 'individualistic' way of viewing the nature of our Self. I view psychosynthesis as an approach that consciously affirms a level of unity into which we awaken once we have individuated. Addressing the subtle level of world view in which we have been steeped as a culture for many years, and how that may be permeating our work as counsellors and psychotherapists, is particularly important when we start addressing the way in which we work in the consulting room. Beyond the vision of the models we learn as students, are we practising an approach that truly elicits a sense of interconnectedness?

Contemporary approaches

Psychosynthesis practitioners, indeed all psychotherapists and counsellors, now operate in a very different world than the one in which the greats, such as Freud, Jung and Assagioli, worked and developed their theories of the psyche. Exponents of many of the different theoretical schools now believe themselves to have a better perspective on 'the truth' of what drives people and how to alleviate psychological and emotional suffering. Yet we increasingly see overlaps between these different theoretical perspectives, and many counselling and psychotherapy courses describe themselves as integrative these days, offering modules in the many theoretical approaches to produce practitioners who can work with the vast array of issues that clients present; clients who are informed and affected by their infinitely varied cultural, religious, economic, and educational backgrounds.

Due to economic pressures on therapeutic services, counselling and psychotherapy is under pressure to be delivered in a short term format, with measurable outcomes produced to justify the funding stream underpinning the service itself. Clients often present in private practice with busy lives and limited funds, asking for quick fixes and time-limited interventions. As life has become more varied and pressurized, the time available has become more limited, leading practitioners to draw upon as many approaches as possible to meet the differing needs and demands of the client groups they are working with.

Models in practice

As a psychotherapist, along with my training in psychosynthesis, I have found the work of Ken Wilber, an American writer on transpersonal psychology with his books *No Boundary: Eastern and Western Approaches to Personal Growth* and the *The Spectrum of Consciousness* (among the many that he has written), to be the most useful in terms of outlining the different levels of consciousness that clients are working on, and the different therapeutic approaches that are the most effective for them. My work has also been informed by the work of Arnold Mindell, the founder of Process Oriented Psychology, which draws on Jungian approaches, Eastern Philosophy, field theory and quantum physics.

As a result of these different influences, I have created a fusion of approaches to map client material that can, in the case of short term work, increase the speed at which a practitioner may assess the client's psychological landscape. Such a hypothesis creates a direction for the work to take, without having to spend many hours of therapeutic time drawing out the autobiographical history that is so often the precursor for any kind of depth work to occur with clients.

While this model might be viewed by many practitioners as simplistic, I have found – as a trainer of groups of practitioners from varied theoretical backgrounds – for it to be extremely useful, mainly because the terminology and language used in this model is 'everyday' language that mimics the terms that clients use to describe themselves, rather than relying on the clinical language of psychotherapy trainings. The change in language is used deliberately to encourage practitioners to de-mystify psychological theory both for themselves and their clients, to level the playing field of the consulting room, and to create a pragmatic and straightforward approach to mapping the issues being presented with a collaborative way forward.

Key client challenges

In my experience the single most consistently presented issue by both clients and therapists is that of challenges with relationship: clients struggle to relate to their parents, siblings, partners, children, work colleagues and friends, while therapists struggle with how to relate to their clients in an authentic, appropriate way. People are often challenged by how to create contactful engagement with others, particularly as many cultures teach people to avoid conflict, play down emotional engagement, and to rely on a cognitive, socially acceptable set of rules that keeps things as safe as possible. The therapeutic culture is no different in that it too teaches students to avoid conflict, play down emotional engagement (on the part of the therapist), and to rely on a cognitive, socially acceptable set of rules that keep things safe.

Given that intimacy and relationship is possibly one of the most challenging issues of our time, I have been interested in developing a model for working that emphasizes the creation of contact, and which encourages the practitioner to become more experientially involved in the work. Field theory tells us that it is impossible to be a neutral observer, and as such, perhaps it is time for psychotherapy to take this on board. Instead of teaching students that they must contain and process experience outside of their client work, with their own therapist and supervisor, trainings could be teaching students how to use their experience whilst they are in the room with their clients.

This of course increases risks of spontaneity, and the resulting anxiety that accompanies it. However, clients seek a practice ground for expressing more of who they are, in the hope of having more meaningful lives and relationships with themselves and others. This practice ground is sought with practitioners who have spent years in therapy training learning to become more self-contained; to deflect personal questions, to strip their consulting rooms of any personal content and to, in effect, become a neutral reflector of the client's material in the belief that if the client is reflected in an appropriate way that they will become more self-accepting.

Unfortunately, the real world of the client does not operate like that; the world around us is critical, secretive, hostile and unsupportive some of the time, so why do we not bring the consulting room more into the real world and create relationships with clients which are more upfront, less 'safe', more unpredictable and honest, with practitioners who can practice with the client how to relate in ways that are authentic and alive? I think that the answer is 'yes', and the themes outlined in the following chapters are aimed at exploring how we, as practitioners, can achieve that relational contact with our clients.

[1] Joseph H. Goodbread, *Radical Intercourse: How dreams unite us in love, conflict and other inevitable relationships* (Portland, OR: Lao Tse Press, 1997).

[2] Jean Hardy, *Psychology with a Soul* (London: Woodgrange Press, 1996), citing Thomas Kuhn, *The Structure of Scientific Revolutions* (1962; Chicago, IL, and London: University of Chicago Press, 1970); Jean Hardy, *There is Another World, but it is This One* (London: QUG, 1988), p. 3.

[3] Roberto Assagioli, *Psychosynthesis* (London: Thorsons, 1965), p. 19.

[4] Diana Whitmore, *Psychosynthesis Counselling in Action* (London: Sage Publications Ltd., 1991), p. 115.

Chapter 2

Concepts of the Self and Relational Space

We turn now to the world of physics in order to deepen our understanding of some of the concepts which were introduced in the last chapter, to examine the shifting paradigms in science and the impact that might have on the way we view the therapeutic relationship.

From Newton to the quantum world

Classical Newtonian physics has three basic tenets:

- Cause and effect; everything happens as a result of something that causes it.

- Determinism: everything is seen to work in a predetermined fashion.

- Wholes are comprised of the sum of their parts (all of which function to make the whole function effectively).

Atoms were presumed to be unchanging and indestructible until the early 20th century when the atom was split, and a number of subatomic particles were identified (now over 100). Subsequently, Einstein developed his theory of relativity and the basic tenets of Newtonian physics were severely rocked. He concluded that instead of space and time being separate entities, they are connected in a way that he called spacetime continuum (curved by the influence of gravity). All objects relate relative to the curved nature of the space-time continuum. Energy and mass were no longer seen as separate, but two aspects of the same phenomena. His theory opened up a world in which mass is not an inanimate, indestructible form, but is instead a living form of energy that is capable of change. Things could now only be understood in relation to each other and interdependently.[1]

Quantum reality

The basic and most impactful statement from quantum physics about matter and therefore the nature of reality is:

> ... that all being at the subatomic level can be described equally well either as solid particles, like so many minute billiard balls, or as waves, like undulations of the surface of the sea. Further, quantum physics goes on to tell us that neither description is really accurate on its own, that both the wavelike and the particlelike aspects of being must be considered when trying to understand the nature of things, and that it is the duality itself that is most basic. Quantum "stuff" is, essentially, both wavelike and particlelike, simultaneously.[2]

Both waves and particles are equally fundamental ways in which matter can manifest itself. 'Wave packets' is the name given to the mixture of the two that make up most subatomic particles. This sense of essential uncertainty replaces the old Newtonian ideas of determinism in which reality is fixed and determined: an electron might express itself as a wave or a particle in any given sphere at any given time.

There are also new perceptions about movement. Movement used to be seen as something quantifiable, consisting of a body of certain density moving at a certain speed through the space defined between the point of departure and the point of arrival. In quantum reality there is no real 'space' between things, and therefore movement is more a series of leaps in which electrons jump from one energy state to another depending on the number of quanta (energy packets) they have absorbed or released. Zohar describes this movement between states very clearly; an electron puts out feelers to all possibilities through a sort of omnipresence in many orbits (as if smeared out over space and time) and then makes a real transition to one of those possibilities. It's as if that electron 'tries out' many different properties in a ghostly way before finally manifesting itself in one way/place. These probability waves therefore describe a vision of reality as full of indefinite possibility stretching out in all directions. There is no separateness and all things and moments touch each other at every point. This accounts for the phenomenon of non-locality at a subatomic level; correlation experiments of pairs of correlated photons show us that two events can be related across time and space in an 'in tune' way (simultaneously). In other words, there is no simple cause and effect, although the extent to which nonlocal influences exist depends on the extent to which the system(s) are in particle or wave states.

In addition to this uncertainty, the way reality expresses itself as either a wave or particle seems dependent on the very act of observation. As a result of Schrodinger's cat experiment (dealt with in detail in Zohar's book, *Quantum Self*) the role of observation was questioned.[3] It appears that there are numerous possible outcomes available until the act of observation, at which point the wave function (which represents this simultaneous existence of many possibilities) collapses and one of the potentials manifests. To complicate things further, an experiment called the Wheeler delayed-choice experiment suggests that whether a photon, for example, behaves as a wave or a particle depends on the way in which we observe. What we expect to happen often elicits that result (if you observe a photon with a particle detector, you will get a particle; likewise, with a wave detector, you get a wave).

Observation and reality

The role of observation in the co-creation of reality raises important questions about the role of the therapist and the powerful impact that their worldviews and unconscious assumptions may have on the outcome of therapy for the client. It behoves us to take even more responsibility to seek out our true expectations. 'Holding the vision', or even the theory, that the client has a larger potential than they are presently identified with, may not be enough if our own deepest beliefs run counter to such a vision.

Zohar disagrees with Capra, Bohr and Heisenberg that this therefore suggests that there is no such thing as objective reality, arguing instead that reality is co-created through a process of interaction. She leans towards a view in which reality does exist, as a vast sea of potential, with which we co-create (rather than simply create as sole authors) to birth or evoke an aspect of the underlying potential at any one time. She argues that we must hold a balanced view that is both particle like and wave like, viewing human beings as being real, separate and solid (the particle aspect of Being) as well as interrelated (the wave aspect of Being).

She goes further to describe the link between electrons and 'reality' (i.e., how does the act of observation 'kill the cat?') as consciousness which has a physical reality to it, arguing that seeing consciousness as a non-physical reality is a part of the old Cartesian model that separates mind and matter. Her quantum mechanical view of consciousness is that consciousness is created in a similar way to the pumped system of electrically charged molecules first described by Herbert Frohlich.[4] When energy is pumped into electrically charged molecules, a threshold of excitation is reached beyond which the molecules begin to vibrate in unison, pulling them into the most ordered form of condensed phase possible – a Bose-Einstein condensate, in which the parts that make up an ordered system allow their identities to overlap. She suggests that this is what creates the background coherence of consciousness or a steady state from which we can have awareness and make choices. Consciousness cannot be traced back to matter as its origin (to the being of a particle). It is instead the relationship between two or more particles; in other words, it is a relational phenomenon.

Interestingly, Zohar argues that the less energy a system has, the less likely it is to be able to draw itself into a condensed state; and that internal conflicts lower the amount of energy available. Her hypothesis is that, like particle systems, our selves are partially integrated systems of subselves that sometimes assert their own identities though their boundaries shift and change as boundaries of excitation within the Bose-Einstein condensate shift and change.

> The selves within selves of the quantum person undulate and overlap, sometimes more, sometime less (each is a quantum wave function), and their region of overlap at any one moment accounts for the sense of "i" at that moment. "I" am an ever-present witness to the dialogues between my selves, the highest unity of all my many subunites. This is the most basic definition of the self at any given moment – the most highly integrated unity of all my many subunities... Each of us as a person is a composite of quantum subselves that are also one self (one highest unity).[5]

This correlates with subpersonality theory in psychosynthesis, although psychosynthesis might disagree that our sense of 'I' develops out of the overlap of the subpersonalities within the psyche, arguing rather that it is something that exists autonomously to our internal parts, as a reflection of Self within the personality. This is an important distinction and again raises the question of how effectively Self can incarnate into the personality without a relational context, within and without of itself. We could hypothesize that the intentional Self chooses to incarnate through the baby (and throughout our whole lives), and that the baby (and adult) needs to lay down the relational wave functions in order to develop the level of cohesiveness through which Self can be experienced and expressed. In other words, the Self is not born out of the overlaps within a personality; it 'is', in and of itself, but needs the cohesiveness of such overlaps through which to incarnate. Both theories are therefore a part of the puzzle.

These theories ask us to reassess the nature of reality, all of which raise potential new ways of addressing relationship. We are brought back to the central questions of how separate and connected we really are. I will expand on Zohar's ideas to this area of relationship, before examining concepts such as the hologram and field theory to look at what connects us.

Connections and overlaps

Just as there are overlaps within our subselves, there are also overlapping wave functions between individuals. We have particle aspects to our natures in which we are defined selves that relate, and we have wave aspects which are the relationships between that which is defined. Both have a common source in quantum reality.

Zohar describes object-relations theory in quantum terms, as a process in which the baby initially merges with the mother's wave function, laying down her responses on his own quantum memory system (and therefore influencing the development of neural pathways in the brain).[6] Next, he begins to also take in others' wave functions, weaving them into his inner complexity until he has completed the task of having integrated many relationships, which give him an experience of coherence and solidity. He feels safe to be both overlapped with mother and feeling that he has other parts that are free for other relationships.

Seeing this process of overlapping as an actuality, whereby the baby takes in the wave pattern reality of others, is subtly different from the model of development that Gila and Firman propose. In *The Primal Wound*, they describe these significant 'others' as external unifying centres who, by their relating to the developing personality, mirror and therefore make cohesive the individual's ability to relate to their own parts empathically. The very language differs from a quantum perspective in that it delineates external and internal, implying a separateness in which others are absorbed as object representations of the baby's own internal I-Self connection.

> As each stage of life is supported and held by the appropriate empathic external unifying centre, active interaction with that external unifying centre conditions the formation of an inner representation or model of that centre, which can be called an internal unifying centre.[7]

Zohar suggests that we go through the process of overlapping wave functions throughout our lives; taking another person into ourselves, allowing ourselves to be changed and integrating that change within a sense of individuality again, as we combine with and create ever larger systems. As wave patterns can overlap, we can 'get inside' each other and form creative, internal relationships. After this meeting, each becomes part of something new that is larger than itself. An identity is maintained through our particle aspects and we merge and intermingle with other wave patterns to create larger identities through our wave aspects. Because wave functions have non-local properties, they can overlap at a distance. This means that we affect each other without having to be close geographically.

> In so many ways, my relationships with others seem but an extension of my relationships with the subselves of my own self, suggesting that any permanent dividing line between myself and others, between the I and the not-I, is not a very meaningful one. There is no clear way to say where "I" end and "you" begin.[8]

The hologram and the field

Another concept within physics which is potentially relevant to psychotherapy is that of the hologram. The idea of the hologram was introduced initially in 1947 by Dennis Gabor, but it wasn't until 1967 that Emmett Leith and Juris Upatrick constructed the first hologram.[9] The essence of the hologram is that the whole is greater than the sum of the parts and that the whole is also contained in each part. This description very much fits the transcendent/immanent nature of the Self as defined by psychosynthesis theory. In 1969, the neurophysiologist Karl Pribram proposed that the human brain functions like a hologram; that its information is not stored or understood locally, but is spread (like a wave) throughout in frequency patterns. Then, in 1971, David Bohm proposed that the Universe itself is holographic, and that everything that unfolds externally (the explicate order) is a fragmented manifestation of an underlying unbroken wholeness (the implicate order). He coined the phrase 'quantum potential' to describe a new field that pervaded all of space. He saw this field/wholeness as being the primary reality which is the source of all life and meaning. 'Despite the apparent separateness of things at the explicate level, everything is a seamless extension of everything else, and ultimately the implicate and explicate orders blend into each other'.[10]

The dreambody

Physicist and psychotherapist Arnold Mindell has his own description of the universal hologram or field, which he calls the 'dreambody'. He says that the universal dreambody '... has field characteristics, behaves in any moment like a hologram, and evolves like an immense human being, or anthropos'.[11] Mindell suggests that one person can 'dream up' another to carry aspects of his personal process for him, as all dynamics operate like holograms in which personal and collective are intermingled, channelled through whoever is most available (due to their particular psychological make-up).

Therefore, we are constantly affected not just by our individual dreambodies, but also by a universal dreambody which is constantly dreaming us into being and expressing ever-larger aspects of itself. The roles in which we find ourselves are always partially affected by the world – by relationship and personal issues within the 'field' at any given time. The areas that we are most open to or have greater personal edges against will define the experiences we tend to identify with or push away. In this way, our identities and experience can never be static or wholly personal, but rather what part of the hologram we are open to experiencing and which we are not, as we interact with it.

All of these concepts imply that in changing ourselves we change the world and that in return our personal problems are influenced by, or even organized by, the development of the larger field in which we live. Mindell suggests that as part of our individuation process we need to relate to the world as if it is a part of us and that we too are part of its development. What these theories have in common is the notion that we are on some level not simply interrelated, but formed and changed by ongoing interactions at a deep level of reality. We are, in some complex way, our relationships. New overlaps and interactions alter my consciousness which in turn lays down and alters the neural pathways in my brain, which in turn affects the way I process and make meaning of reality. Each relationship changes who I am.

Zohar speaks of relationships in the deepest sense, not just to others but to all living things (whose cells contain quantum systems) and to transpersonal qualities with which we share the common quality of creating relationship. We are all basically made of the same stuff.

> In my own being, which draws its very existence from the creation of relational wholes, I am by nature a creature that is stuff of the same substance as love, truth, and beauty. Not because I create them, but because the nature of my own consciousness is synonymous with the nature of their meaning. Through my own being I have the capacity to act as midwife to their expression in this world, and they in turn mould and make the self that I am.[12]

These theories urge us to commit to these relationships and to allow ourselves to be entangled as we interweave new wholes. In fact, to deepen my central core, it may be imperative that I allow myself to deeply enter and be changed by intimate relationship with others, my environment and spiritual values.

Presence

Within psychosynthesis we often speak of presence as being of vital importance to the relationship. The ideas explored in this chapter seem to urge us to think of presence as an interactive phenomena in which we get inside of our clients and them inside of us, to allow ourselves to be affected and changed by them. Self can be seen as the 'implicate order' or quantum level of potential to which we can open ourselves by moving beyond any ideas we may have of the work being solely about the client and about the client's issues. Whilst we have a degree of individuality, it seems that individuation is achieved not by focusing on 'my self-fulfilment' or even 'my self-actualization' in which concern for others follows work on myself, but in which collective and relational concerns are the forum in which I truly discover myself. If Self is quantum, then it seems to be expressed and experienced in the quality of interaction occurring between therapist and client (and their worlds) at every moment. Following the quantum approach, the client needs to become entangled with us to generate a stronger and firmer sense of self as each intermingling of wave patterns forms an evermore cohesive overlap of wave patterns within themselves.

Personal and transpersonal presence

Firman and Gila, in *The Primal Wound*, describe the Self as a personal presence as well as a transpersonal one. The Self is not just a personal and collective unconscious from which all experience flows, but it is a presence and reality that knows us intimately and acts through the transpersonal Will to make an impact on our lives. 'Self is not a blind, impersonal totality....'[13] This is an important distinction that differentiates psychosynthesis theory from models which go no further than identifying a collective unconscious which impacts us, extending this bigger context to include a source of infinite Being and intentionality that acts through the collective field. This collective field contains patterns of experience and relationship that 'we' the collective are working with, in our evolutionary process of encompassing broader and more refined expressions of Self incarnating.

Relational context

Let us now return to Firman and Gila's description of the task of the therapist as one of establishing empathic connections with the client by becoming an external unifying centre through which we can be a channel for the flow of Being from Self to the client's 'I'.

Firman and Gila's approach to the development of greater Self realization as occurring within a relational context is one that concurs with the scientific theories I have been exploring; that true development of a meaningful, connected experience of life can only occur within the facilitating relationships of relevant 'others', whether communities of our families, nature, mystical community or geographical community. However, their description of this connection is still one which views individual awareness as separate, albeit connected from a ground of Being (Self) through which empathic connections can flow, and that our relationship to each other is one of internalized representations.[14] It utilizes a concept of field in which one part of a field can cause effects in other parts of the field.

Quantum theory takes the concept of empathic connection/resonance further by suggesting that it is not just object representations or models that we take in, nor that our own process is stimulated by the other (like stimulating like). Rather, it is that the coming together of these two people forms new relational wholes that are physical realities – taken fully into ourselves, changing the wave functions and patterns within us and altering the network of neurons through which we organize information and perceive reality. In quantum fields, there are no well-defined causes for events. There are instead potentials for manifestations in spacetime. Quantum fields express a profound interconnectedness, which we can only understand if we release old notions of independently existent objects causally interacting.

Towards wholeness

Interestingly, Firman and Gila describe the journey of Self realization to be a process whereby the middle unconscious broadens to include ever more of the higher and lower unconscious. So that the field of awareness is able to engage with all experiences as they arise; a wholeness based on openness to all experience rather than on a pattern of unity. This is a wonderful image that describes the task of life as one in which we are able to flow with whatever is present, in a way that is both fully in the experience and yet also more than that experience. This image reminds me of the dream with which I began this book.

The collective unconscious

I would add to it the significant point stressed by Assagioli: that we are also open to a collective unconscious and thus much of our personal experience may not just be 'our own'. Therefore a willingness is required to embrace and facilitate the processing of material that is also collective.

The collective may well need people who are open to and able to process certain themes; particularly ones that are outside of our cultural norms and which are largely marginalized or denied by the majority of people. If indeed we are part of a holographic or quantum process whereby we are impacted constantly by others, then it would make sense to hypothesize that the global field will seek out available channels or 'processors' for certain conflicts. Maybe those of us who are open to working with these issues are used by the Self to process them for the collective (thereby also developing and expanding our own range of interaction within our field of awareness).

Individuation to interdependence

This brings the concept of service into the work that we do with clients in a very immediate way and deepens the meaningful nature of every interaction that we have; turning from a narcissistically 'me' focused attitude of self development, to one which sees the larger function of Self realization as an ability to engage with life (and all life forms) in an ever broadening, present way. In this respect it becomes less important (both as a therapist and a client) to ask 'is this your stuff or mine?', but to simply engage with what is, from a place of Self that can be empathically present to it as relevant and important no matter who it 'belongs' to. Thus, individuation moves away from a process of defining myself as distinct from you, towards a process of developing an ability to engage with the present moment in its widest sense, as an interdependent, dynamic interaction in which I am fully a part of the collective and my contribution is the quality of my presence that I can bring to it at any given moment.

Clinical application

The ideas that we have been exploring are both large – in that they expand our minds on the nature of reality – and also particular, in that they address the very intimate nature of the immanent moment between therapist and client. Now let's begin to play with the theory to see how it might facilitate interaction in the therapy room.

Boundaries and 'potential space'

At this point, it is important to look at the value of boundaries. We speak often of the need for boundaries as a way of making it safe for the client to explore themselves and their environment. D. W. Winnicott's ideas about boundary and space are very useful in identifying how the two interact. He postulated that form and boundaries are needed in order to give the content meaning. In therapy we provide a time and space boundary which frames a moment of a person's experience in much the same way as an artist does when he faces a blank canvas. Within this space the client (and I would say, the therapist) feels safe enough to allow spontaneity and play. This reflects the individual's development of 'potential space' offered by the holding environment in the early months of life (by mother and father).

Winnicott's phrase 'potential space' describes the overlap between our inner and outer realities, which he calls a third area that is simultaneously the world of our inner dreams and the outside world of shared reality. He hypothesized that this third space is neither one nor the other, neither is it 'between' people, but is a space in which meaning is made through creativity and symbol formation. The 'potential space' addresses the nature of interaction, which is occurring where

... we are neither inside in the world of dream and fantasy nor outside in the world of shared reality. We are in the paradoxical third place that partakes of both these places at once.[15]

Schwartz-Salant, a Jungian analyst, also speaks about this third space which he calls the subtle body. He asserts that the subtle body can only be perceived through imagination and that it is through the subtle body that transference and its transformation passes. He refers to Winnicott's idea of potential space as an important concept but extends it to view this field (or subtle body) as '... a field occupied with its own processes'.[16]

Schwartz-Salant suggests that every complex (or sub-personality in psychosynthesis theory) has a body which is neither wholly a physical or a mental structure, but an 'in between phenomenon' which can manifest in many experiential channels. Within the therapeutic relationship there can be an overlap of these subtle bodies between therapist and client. This creates a process of kinship in which a Self structure is formed between two people, through which deep transformative processes can be released. He says that this kinship often occurs unconsciously in therapy but can be worked with consciously through active imagination to unfold the experience occurring between therapist and client. He seems to do this by feeling very closely the experience he is having, which often means identifying with one of the figures in a couple emerging in the subtle body (the subtle body being full of relational phenomena) and then describing this experience or speaking directly from it. The client then joins him in this interaction, in which the use of imaginal sight (visualization) is transformative, often contacting much deeper and more profound processes than would be available through the exploration of transference in the form of taking back transference projections.

The central issue is that, contrary to the spirit where the individual Self is regarded as the pearl of great price, a Self can be created between, and of, two people without a negative participation mystique domination and without either person losing identity. With the proper use of imagination and, integrated experience... two people can experience the Self and return to this Self again and again... The same uplifting spirit, order, wisdom, and gnosis can be gained from this Self.[17]

Interestingly, though this sounds like working with projective identification phenomena in which the client is thought to project split off parts of themselves that they cannot integrate onto the therapist, then acting towards the therapist as though they are those split off parts, Schwartz-Salant makes a distinction between the two approaches. He says that projective identification utilizes a Cartesian, causal metaphor which contains the idea of parts and a spatial model which has a clear inside and outside. Whereas the utilization of a subtle body concept sees client and therapist entering a different space which is composed of relationships rather than projected parts. He compares this relational space with Bohm's idea of the implicate order from which space-time processes evolve, which is dominated by relations and which can be linked to, by the use of imaginal sight.

By focusing upon processes in this third area, experienced as an interactive field, and not reducing them to projections that must be withdrawn, two people can apprehend a variety of linking structures, notably fusion, distance, and union.[18]

In this respect, it is not so important which parts belong to whom, as therapist and client gain awareness of the linkage structures that have been dominating the interaction. Schwartz-Salant is keen to point out that this is not fusing with the client, which is often characterized by a nondifferentiation of the process between two people. Instead, it is an experience of unity in which awareness is brought to the quality of interaction occurring in the creative moment. This links to Winnicott's argument that it is only through the ability to engage in potential space activities (characterized by relational phenomena) that true individuation can occur, as the individual is free to make meaning and therefore operate as a mature member of society; able to make creative contributions rather than operate as a victim of others' values/opinions or as an oppressor towards others.

Interactive field perspectives

In their article 'On the Physics and Psychology of the Transference as an Interactive Field', Jungian analyst J. M. Spiegelman and physicist V. Mansfield propose that there is a stage of working in which the therapist and client seem to be structured by the field condition (which, for them, is mediated by archetypes within the collective unconscious).[19] In this phase, therapist and client have simultaneous imagery or sensations which describe a particular process that is trying to emerge. For example, Spiegelman was working with a priest who suffered from depression, unalleviated through previous analysis. Spiegelman noticed that he was having strong images of kneeling with the client before a Durer print of *Christ Crowned with Thorns*. He shared this with the client who immediately wanted to do this and together they prayed. During this experience of prayer, they had simultaneous body experiences of being touched on the shoulders by a Christ-like presence. This moment marked a reconnection for the man with his inner priestly vocation.

Spiegelman and Mansfield suggest that this is often one stage within the work and is not an intensity that is present all the time. They assert that this is a slightly different way of working with transference because the transference model suggests causal phenomena in which the client's projected contents affect the therapist, who either forms an empathic intervention from this information, silently or verbally making an interpretation of what this projection might mean for the client, or, through the therapist's ability to sustain and integrate the difficult content, creates a change in the system by handing it back to the patient in a more digestible form.

They describe the constellation of an interactive field as

acausal, synchronistic and meaning making, in which we abandon the idea that all events have a defined cause. At this level, there are often meaningful correlations of images and simultaneous sensations which argue for viewing the experience as an acausal expression of meaning rather than as a causal influence between therapist and client. They assert that if we want to participate in the field, our sense of separate identity must diminish to allow an openness to imagination, feelings and intuitions rather than linear thought processes that seek to understand rather than be immersed in the process. They, like Schwartz-Salant, work with this phenomenon using active imagination (often mutual imagination shared verbally as it is occurring with both therapist and client), close attention to physical sensations, and utilizing role-playing if that seems appropriate.

Dreambody and awareness

Whilst Schwartz-Salant, Spiegelman and Mansfield utilize the imagination to enter this 'third field' of interactive phenomena (or we could postulate, quantum phenomena), Arnold Mindell has identified several experiential channels in which the implicate order can be unfolded. He advocates techniques for developing a 'second attention' which can notice the irrational, or unusual events, and which signals the dreambody (implicate order) is at work. The 'first attention' relates to the primary reality of everyday life, much like making sure there is a captain at the helm of a ship, but the secondary attention is needed to bring forth the potential that is attempting to emerge. In this respect we can be in several places at once: both here and now in space-time and accessing the quantum field in which many possibilities lie. He likens this to the shamanistic role of traditional tribal cultures, where the shaman was required to leave everyday reality and journey to other worlds to speak with or wrestle with the spirits behind physical reality to keep them from impinging on the tribe. For the shaman there are spirits behind all of life, which we, if we can relate to them, can co-create with.

Mindell, like Spiegelman and Mansfield, sees the global dream-body as a noncausal field with synchronistic connections organized by patterns without any known outside influence on the parts. In this respect, there are processes 'dreaming' the client and therapist into being constantly. If we are to work effectively, we must watch with a second attention to help the psyche to awareness, which in his view will do whatever is necessary to reorganize itself creatively, with or without our conscious participation. In other words, we will suffer from our symptoms if we do not consciously cooperate with them. He too advocates dropping an attachment to a personal identity or history that limits who you are in the moment and shuts off relevant (but denied) avenues of experience.

> Finally the point arrives when the more you change, the more you sense the complexity of it all. Changing identities, even becoming free from a previous inhibition, is not enough. The process of creating and dropping personal history leads to the discovery that you are neither this nor that, but the awareness of it all... During such difficult times, you are forced to undo yourself, to go to pieces, to free yourself from the tendency to think of yourself at any given time as one type of person with one type of task. Either you become fluid, or nature erases you in its own way.[20]

Mindell's outline of the channels in which secondary phenomena can unfold include: visual, auditory, proprioceptive (physical sensation), kinaesthetic (movement), relationships, the world (wider environment.) In any of these channels of experience problematic symptoms can cause us trouble, usually in the channels which are least occupied (less known to us). The advice is to unfold the experience in the channel in which it is occurring, either in the client or within ourselves as therapists, as we identify with dream figures within the field and interact with the client from this place **with awareness**. This dual awareness is extremely important in Process Work and is also emphasized by Schwartz-Salant; that to avoid acting out or merging, the therapist must bring awareness to the process that is occurring and metacommunicate about the experience whilst it is happening. This is similar to the concept of maintaining an 'I' awareness in psychosynthesis, which is present with, but not 'had' by the experience. In other words, to identify oneself as 'that which is having the experience' whilst staying in contact with the phenomenology.

Dreaming up

On writing about process oriented psychology, Joe Goodbread, in his book *Radical Intercourse*, calls the process of transference/countertransference 'dreaming up'.[21] Dreaming up is a process which is mediated by dream figures (personifications of experience), which behave like personalities. It is governed by the channels of experience which a person is open to and by the personal edges of therapist and client. We are often either dreamed up to be figures with whom we are either comfortable, or figures that represent a way of being that we deny. He sees dreaming up as the product of the dream field present (consisting of the individual's psychology and something more than that, the universal field), as a larger pattern trying to express itself through the people present.

Within Goodbread's frame of reference we can view the dream figures we are called to embody with clients as a part of the field that has a will to incarnate, and which will use the most available resource within which to do so; sometimes eliciting the use of the therapist, or channels of experience over which the client has little control because they do not inhabit that. Goodbread advocates role-playing with clients from these dream figures (whilst maintaining metacommunication) to allow the client to move their process into the here and now. From a field perspective, the mythology within the field itself is full of relational phenomena that wish to be unfolded and incarnated and these will utilize the work between therapist to client as an arena in which to manifest. From this perspective, it is more than the client's or the therapist's material coming through from the unconscious, but many patterns for relating with universal themes.

Figure 1. Assagioli's egg model of the psyche.

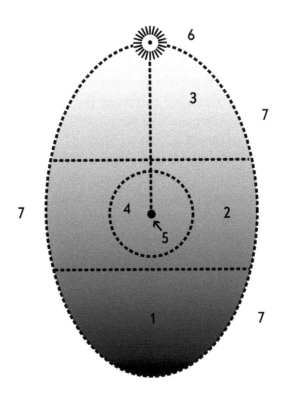

1. THE LOWER UNCONSCIOUS
2. THE MIDDLE UNCONSCIOUS
3. THE HIGHER UNCONSCIOUS OR SUPERCONSCIOUS
4. THE FIELD OF CONSCIOUSNESS
5. THE CONSCIOUS SELF OR "I"
6. THE HIGHER SELF
7. THE COLLECTIVE UNCONSCIOUS

ASSAGIOLI'S EGG MODEL

Relationship dynamics and Self
as an organizing principle

My own hypothesis about the relational, or quantum, field with which we are seeking to engage is that the Self is an organizing principle which mediates the collective field and relational experiences unfolding within and between people. The relationship between and within client and therapist is therefore full of Self 'in potential'. Whilst it is somewhat unrepresentative to depict causal flows of effects in my diagrams, it seems helpful to break down the interaction of Self and personality. However, I would see these effects as operating much more synchronistically and acausally at a quantum level. I use the following diagrams to depict potential relationship dynamics. Figure 1 is Assagioli's original egg model. Diagram A is my adaption of Assagioli's original egg diagram of the psyche (Figure 2). Diagram B examines the dynamic between Self, collective and psyche with an example (Figure 3). Diagram C takes a closer look at the relational phenomena occurring between therapist and client (Figures 4.1 and 4.2).

Subpersonalities as holographic microcosms

In diagram A (Figure 2), I show the collective unconscious archetypal patterns influencing the individual psyche. The Self is both the source of all phenomena (transcendent aspect of Self) and the core of it, at the heart of every experience (immanent aspect of Self). The higher, middle and lower unconscious become representations of the depth to which we are willing to make contact with the present moment (and the experiences within that moment). The more contactful we are able to be with our inner and outer relationships, the more purely we experience Self, and the more personally we are touched by Self – rather than being inflated by the grandeur of Self.

I am therefore hypothesizing that subpersonalities (as microcosms of the whole psyche) become emissaries of the Self – differentiated facets of the Self carrying particular qualities, purpose and function; vehicles through which the Self incarnates. If each

Figure 2. Diagram A, author's adaptation
of Assagioli's egg model of the psyche.

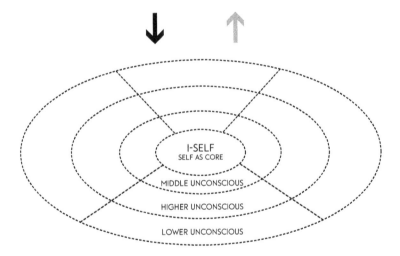

SELF AS SOURCE

ARCHETYPAL PATTERNS
IN COLLECTIVE UNCONSCIOUS

I-SELF
SELF AS CORE

MIDDLE UNCONSCIOUS

HIGHER UNCONSCIOUS

LOWER UNCONSCIOUS

SUBPERSONALITY AS HOLOGRAM REFLECTING
THE WHOLE PSYCHE (SAME STRUCTURE)

SELF AS FIELD

DIAGRAM A.

SHOWS THE DIFFERENT FUNCTIONS OF SELF, SENDING INFLUENCES THROUGH THE
COLLECTIVE UNCONSCIOUS TO BE DIFFERENTIATED AT SUBPERSONALITY LEVEL. THE MORE
CONTACTFUL THE PERSONALITY IS ABLE TO BE WITH THESE INFLUENCES, THE MORE FULLY
THEY ARE MANIFESTED AND DIFFERENTIATED: AND THE MORE COMPLETELY SELF IS
EXPERIENCED AND EXPRESSED (WHAT IS NOT MADE CONTACT WITH, REMAINS AS UNCONSCIOUS
MATERIAL). THIS EXPERIENCE INFORMS AND REVERBERATES WITHIN SELF AS SOURCE.

Figure 3. Diagram B, the dynamic between Self, collective and psyche.

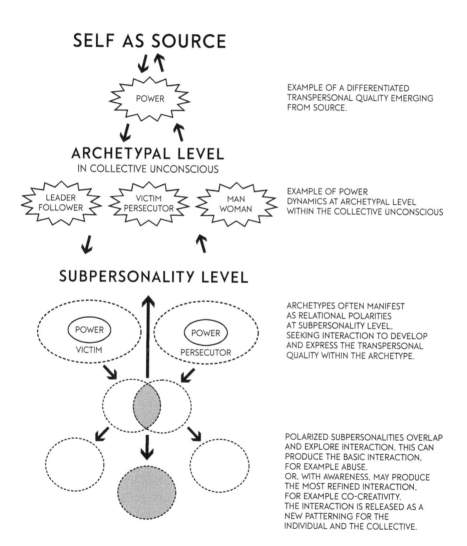

SELF AS SOURCE

EXAMPLE OF A DIFFERENTIATED TRANSPERSONAL QUALITY EMERGING FROM SOURCE.

ARCHETYPAL LEVEL
IN COLLECTIVE UNCONSCIOUS

EXAMPLE OF POWER DYNAMICS AT ARCHETYPAL LEVEL WITHIN THE COLLECTIVE UNCONSCIOUS

SUBPERSONALITY LEVEL

ARCHETYPES OFTEN MANIFEST AS RELATIONAL POLARITIES AT SUBPERSONALITY LEVEL, SEEKING INTERACTION TO DEVELOP AND EXPRESS THE TRANSPERSONAL QUALITY WITHIN THE ARCHETYPE.

POLARIZED SUBPERSONALITIES OVERLAP AND EXPLORE INTERACTION. THIS CAN PRODUCE THE BASIC INTERACTION, FOR EXAMPLE ABUSE.
OR, WITH AWARENESS, MAY PRODUCE THE MOST REFINED INTERACTION, FOR EXAMPLE CO-CREATIVITY.
THE INTERACTION IS RELEASED AS A NEW PATTERNING FOR THE INDIVIDUAL AND THE COLLECTIVE.

DIAGRAM B.
EXAMPLE OF THE SELF INCARNATING THE TRANSPERSONAL QUALITY OF POWER

subpersonality is viewed as a wave pattern, it can be seen as something that is free-floating within, or emerging from, the field between therapist and client (under the direction of Self), as one of many potential outcomes. Maybe, through close observation of our experience and our clients, with appropriate communication about the emerging experience (which is often at the edge of awareness, manifesting as unusual signals, disturbances, sensations, and images), we begin to connect with the many possibilities, eventually collapsing the wave function that we choose to engage with.

Diagram B (Figure 3) depicts the relationship between the different levels of Self. In this diagram I am differentiating archetypes as universal or collective patterns of being and relating, theorizing that subpersonalities are personal patterns of being and relating. The Self can employ both in order to incarnate in a variety of differentiated ways. So, whilst some of what we might be exchanging within a session with clients have subpersonality characteristics, it might also be the case that there are archetypal patterns present that are being picked up and worked through by subpersonalities which 'humanize' these collective patterns. Self is the field from which archetypes and subpersonalities come, the vehicle through which they incarnate, and the core at the heart of each experience.

Relational wholes

Figures 4.1 and 4.2 depict the new relational whole that may be available to the individual personality and larger collective when the therapeutic relationship is contactful with transpersonal qualities. Simultaneously the Self evolves as new relational wholes are explored. Following the holographic and quantum paradigm, each change in the part generates change in the whole and each interaction creates new relational wholes that are more than the sum of the parts. The more overlaps and interaction the client experiences, the greater the experience of 'I-Self' as the place in which contact occurs.

This interpersonal process also reflects an intrapsychic one in which an individual's subpersonalities overlap and through their

Figure 4.1. Relational phenomena between therapist and client.

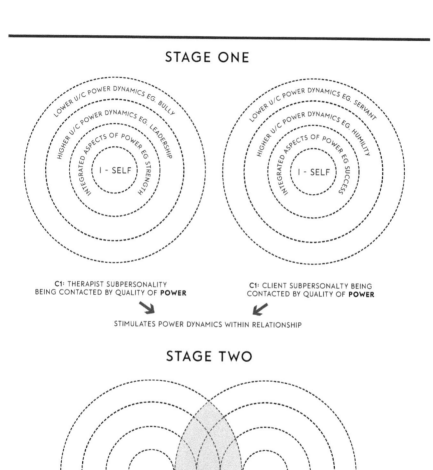

STAGE ONE

C1: THERAPIST SUBPERSONALITY
BEING CONTACTED BY QUALITY OF **POWER**

C1: CLIENT SUBPERSONALTY BEING
CONTACTED BY QUALITY OF **POWER**

STIMULATES POWER DYNAMICS WITHIN RELATIONSHIP

STAGE TWO

C2: SUBPERSONALITIES ACT LIKE OVERLAPPING WAVES. THE MORE OVERLAPPED THEY ARE,
THE DEEPER AND FULLER THE CONTACT, COVERING ALL AREAS OF THE RELATIONAL DYNAMIC OF POWER.

DIAGRAM C. DETAILED DIAGRAM OF WHAT OCCURS AT THE SUBPERSONALITY LEVEL
IN DIAGRAM B. WITHIN THE THERAPEUTIC RELATIONSHIP

Figure 4.2, continued. Relational phenomena between therapist and client.

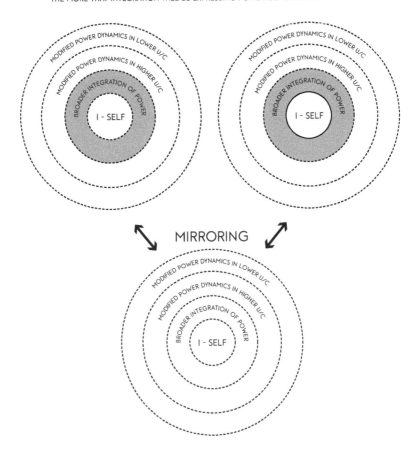

STAGE THREE

C3: THERAPIST AND CLIENT SUBPERSONALITIES HAVING INTEGRATED NEW INFORMATION ABOUT POWER RELATIONSHIPS. THE MORE CONTACTFUL THE OVERLAP HAS BEEN, THE MORE THAT INTEGRATION WILL BE EXPRESSING POWER CONSCIOUSLY.

MIRRORING

C4: NEW RELATIONAL PATTERN/QUANTUM SYSTEM EMERGES AS A WHOLE, IN AND OF ITSELF, FROM THE INTERACTION, MIRRORING THE NEW AWARENESS OF POWER DYNAMICS WITHIN THE THERAPEUTIC RELATIONSHIP. THIS PATTERN IS NOW AVAILABLE TO THE COLLECTIVE FIELD AND AFFECTS ARCHETYPAL PATTERNS WHILST ALSO RE-INFORMING SELF. SELF HAS DIFFERENTIATED, EXPLORED ITSELF VIA RELATIONAL PHENOMENA AND EVOLVED AS A RESULT.

DIAGRAM C. CONTINUED

relationships find new ways forward. I think that it is important to stress that overlaps and contact are not necessarily about feeling good, warm or loving, but in being contactful with whatever is present. Goodbread comments, '... Dreaming up binds some of us to one another with cords of silk, and others with barbed wire. Unity does not distinguish between the nice and the nasty; if it has a goal, it is to have us live the fullness of our experience'.[22] However, as I have mentioned previously, the experience of contacting the core of any process may connect to a deep and healing experience of Self that is itself transformative.

Opening to the experience

The common distortion that I would see emerging from this way of working is the tendency to disown all experience as 'from the field' and therefore not really 'mine'. Individuals are often more willing to say challenging things within a group than they would be one to one. The danger here is not facing conflict and challenge as one individual to another. As Mindell comments, 'Taking responsibility means accepting everything you say, feel, hear, write, see, and communicate as part of you'.[23]

This means opening to what is occurring as an experience – no matter who, what or where it originated from – as relevant and meaningful to you, and to engage as closely with that experience as possible, to be at the heart of it, where Self is experienced as immanent and deeply personal. This process, whilst requiring an ability to maintain awareness of the overall process with a meta-communicating 'I' function, often involves momentary loss of clarity, or a sense of entering the chaos. This can be hard for us as therapists, as we are afraid of hurting the client, re-enacting unhelpful roles, or getting lost in the process.

Knowing one's edges

These are important considerations. I come back to Winnicott's concept of the vital presence of boundaries and structure that make it safe enough to follow instincts. There are certain boundaries of behaviour that should be maintained within the therapeutic alliance and following the present moment should not include simply expressing anything that is occurring within you as a therapist. To do so is a sacrifice of awareness and unlikely to be helpful to the client. On a similar note, Schwartz-Salant expresses hesitancy at sharing his working methodology for fear of criticism for holding too loose boundaries. Spiegelman and Mansfield appreciate the difficulties of trying to bring physics to bear on the complexities of the therapeutic relationship. Goodbread expresses the opinion that field theory might not help when looking at everyday human interactions if these theories suffer from a seduction into harmony or lacking sufficient detail for working with the complex psychology of interaction.

I would suggest that a therapist needs to have an ability to know his or her own edges, as well as a capacity to notice the overall process as much as possible whilst following unusual states. This requires a capacity to be both particlelike and wavelike simultaneously, or at least an ability to oscillate between the two states; maintaining a firm here and now containing presence, whilst entering the process. This is certainly something that sounds like an ideal and it is possible to make more mistakes following an interactive approach that favours involvement. However, it is my experience that clients come to therapy to learn how to have relationships, including 'getting into trouble' and how to ride conflicts as well as harmony as an expression of dynamic interaction and intimacy.

Viewing what is occurring as acausal opens us to a wider range of potentialities as therapists. Attitude and core beliefs regarding the essential nature of life affects the nature of the therapeutic encounter. I believe that having a solid grasp of theory is very important, providing an inner structure within which to think about what is going on, reflecting and loosening up any stuck identifications we may have with the material that a client is presenting. However, being able to flow with a process internally and externally without understanding it seems crucial to embracing a quantum perspective in the way we work as therapists. As therapists, we are particlelike from the perspective of 'I am here, being aware' rather than operating from an identity that is based on roles and content, allowing us to move as fluidly wavelike as possible in the moment, noticing the many potentialities that are present: the many faces of the Self. This capacity for creative, interactive experience is essential to health for both client and therapist.

Davis and Wallbridge echo that Winnicott adhered to this definition of health:

> Life, as we know, included for him the idea of richness of quality – of the capacity to be enriched that comes from an intensity of "life experience"... "we are poor indeed if we are only sane". In fact, he found that there were individuals "so firmly anchored in objective reality that they are ill in the direction of being out of touch with the subjective world and with the creative approach to fact." Such people need help because "they feel estranged from dream."[24]

[1] Diarmuid O'Murchu, *Quantum theology: Spiritual implications of the new physics* (Dublin: Gill and Macmillan Ltd., 1997), pp. 24 – 26.

[2] Danah Zohar and Ian N. Marshall, *The Quantum Self: Human nature and consciousness defined by the new physics* (New York: William Morrow and Company, Inc., 1990), p. 25.

[3] Zohar and Marshall, *The Quantum Self*, pp. 30 – 49.

[4] Herbert Frohlich, 'Evidence for Bose condensation-like excitation of coherent modes in biological systems', *Physics Letters A* (Elsevier) 51, no. 1 (1975), pp. 21 – 22.

[5] Zohar and Marshall, *The Quantum Self*, pp. 114 – 133.

[6] Zohar and Marshall, *The Quantum Self*, pp. 135 – 136.

[7] John Firman and Ann Gila, *The Primal Wound: A transpersonal view of trauma, addiction, and growth* (New York: State University of New York Press, 1997), p. 76.

[8] Zohar and Marshall, *The Quantum Self*, p. 139.

[9] O'Murchu, *Quantum theology*, pp. 55.

[10] O'Murchu, *Quantum theology*, pp. 58.

[11] Arnold Mindell, *Coma: The dreambody near death*, 2nd edn (London: Penguin Books Ltd., 1987), p. 98.

[12] Zohar and Marshall, *The Quantum Self*, p. 164.

[13] John Firman and Ann Gila, *The Primal Wound: A transpersonal view of trauma, addiction, and growth* (New York: State University of New York Press, 1997), p. 43.

[14] Firman and Gila, *The Primal Wound*, p. 18.

[15] Madeleine Davis and David Wallbridge, *Boundaries and Space: An introduction to the work of D.W. Winnicott* (London: H. Karnac Books Ltd., 1981), p. 160.

[16] Nathan Schwartz-Salant, *The Borderline Personality: Vision and healing* (Wilmette, IL: Chiron Publications, 1989), p. 7.

[17] Nathan Schwartz-Salant and Murray Stein, eds, *Transference and Countertransference* (Wilmette, IL: Chiron Publications, 1984), pp. 8 – 9.

[18] Schwartz-Salant, *The Borderline Personality*, p. 110.

[19] Victor Mansfield and J. Marvin Spiegelman, 'On the Physics and Psychology of the Transference as an Interactive Field', *Journal of Analytical Psychology* 41, no. 2 (1996), pp. 179 – 202.

[20] Amy Mindell and Arnold Mindell, *Metaskills: The spiritual art of therapy* (Tempe, AZ: New Falcon Publications, 1993), p. 48.

[21] Joseph H. Goodbread, Radical Intercourse: *How dreams unite us in love, conflict and other inevitable relationships* (Portland, OR: Lao Tse Press, 1997).

[22] Goodbread, *Radical Intercourse*, p. 164.

[23] Mindell and Mindell, *Metaskills*, p. 52.

[24] Davis and Wallbridge, *Boundaries and Space*, p. 163.

Chapter 3

Working at the Edge of Awareness

The field of awareness and the unconscious

Having explored the context and influences on the therapeutic relationship and the way in which transference can be described by physics, let's now focus on the part of the client's psyche that is most important for the therapist to relate to. Looking again at Assagioli's egg model, we are going to zoom in to work in the area that he called 'the field of consciousness'. In ordinary language, this is the area that clients describe when they tell a therapist who they are, how they feel, what they believe; in other words, this is the fraction of the psyche that the client is aware of.

This is the central circle of Assagioli's egg model, which is small in comparison to the much larger areas on the model that are the unconscious areas of the psyche. Thus, when a client describes 'who they believe themselves to be', they are often unaware of the vast amount of their psyche that is beyond their conscious awareness.

As a concept, 'the unconscious' is bandied around in everyday conversation, but it is still the case that many people believe that they are fully aware of themselves, and that there is really nothing going on inside of themselves that they are not 'conscious' of. This belief is one of the first challenges for therapists when working with a new client; that if they are not aware of certain feelings, wounds, blueprints and beliefs, they assume that the content must not exist. 'I don't feel it/know it, therefore it isn't in me'. And it is this introduction to the reality and autonomous power of the unconscious that is the most important element of psychoeducation during the course of therapy.

I will be describing the area that Assagioli termed the 'field of consciousness' as the 'field of awareness', because it is full of experiential material that a person has some comfort with, and usu-

Figure 5. Assagioli's egg model.

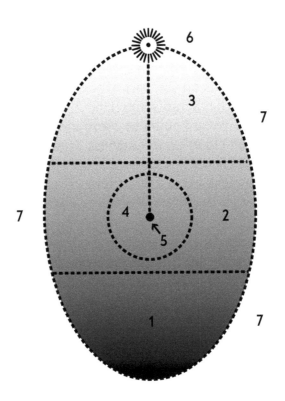

1. THE LOWER UNCONSCIOUS
2. THE MIDDLE UNCONSCIOUS
3. THE HIGHER UNCONSCIOUS OR SUPERCONSCIOUS
4. THE FIELD OF CONSCIOUSNESS
5. THE CONSCIOUS SELF OR "I"
6. THE HIGHER SELF
7. THE COLLECTIVE UNCONSCIOUS

ASSAGIOLI'S EGG MODEL

ally this material is what they present when they describe who they think they are and how they think others see them; in other words, who they are aware of being. The field of awareness can therefore be seen as a person's sense of identity. I like to call it 'the front of house' or that which we present to the world. Some schools of thought call this the survival personality, meaning that it contains the versions of ourselves that we believe we have to be, in order to be accepted in the world.

Psychosynthesis traditionally calls both the preferred and denied parts of ourselves 'subpersonalities'. These are similar to Jung and Freud's theories on 'complexes'. This psychoanalytic term describes a cluster of beliefs, emotions, memories and drives that are organized around a common theme.[1] The psychosynthesis concept of subpersonalities is very similar. Diana Whitmore describes subpersonalities as 'autonomous configurations within the personality as a whole. They are psychological identities, coexisting as a multitude of lives within one person; each with its own specific behaviour pattern and corresponding self-image, body posture, feelings and beliefs'.[2]

Me/Not Me

It is useful to begin to understand which 'parts of ourselves' we are comfortable with and which we are not. Usually, the parts that we are comfortable with exist in the field of awareness, which forms an identity that we are both at home with and which we show to the world. If we think about the psyche as a metaphorical city, there will be many different communities, including authorities, government, and a police force that enforce the rules and regulations of what is considered to be acceptable behaviour. Within the city there will be the acceptable members of the overall community that uphold the status quo, and there will be the unacceptable members. Within the psyche, just as within our cities, the unacceptable members are usually kept separate from the acceptable members, usually through economic circumstance and religious and social preferences and trends. Within the psyche these unacceptable members of our psychological community are contained, suppressed and repressed into the unconscious, the territory that Assagioli described as the middle, higher and lower unconscious. These denied members form marginalized communities within the unconscious, where they exist 'out of sight and out of mind' until they become disgruntled and begin to create an uprising from the unconscious, much like an invasion seeking to cross the boundary, the 'edge', between the unconscious into the field of conscious awareness. It is at that point that people usually come into therapy.

The edge of awareness

It is on this edge of the field of awareness that the therapist and client will spend a lot of time 'camping out'. I see this edge as being similar to the walls of a city, within which acceptable members of the community live, keeping the outliers at bay outside the city walls. These perimeters are usually patrolled in the psyche as 'edge figures'; policing figures of the psyche that seek to keep the troubled parts of the community (the unconscious) out and away from the acceptable parts of the community (the field of awareness). Below is a diagram (Figure 6) that highlights the field of awareness; my names for the acceptable figures/parts inside the field of awareness are 'Me' – that which I find acceptable and how I choose to define myself. The name that I will give to the unacceptable figures that are kept outside of the city walls in the unconscious marginalized communities are 'Not Me' – that which I find unacceptable and deny inside of myself.

Mapping psychological landscape

What I most frequently find when working with students in psychotherapy trainings is that, although they understand the concept of the unconscious, they are more interested in seeing the unconscious as being full of traumatic wounds that must be sought out and worked with, rather than seeing it as a landscape of mystery. We live in times where the therapeutic community are very keen on seeking out trauma, and whilst the unconscious is

Figure 6. Diagram of the Field of Awareness, 'Me' vs 'Not Me'.

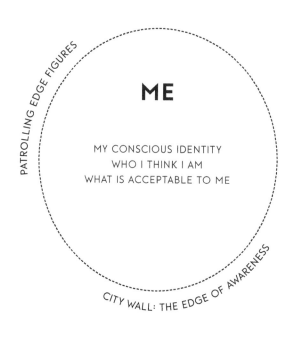

territory that does indeed have wounding within it, it is also full of edges that are demarcated with ideas of right and wrong and defined by a complex matrix of core beliefs and tribal rules that are inherited from many sources. These include family of origin, cultural, religious, educational and legal rules and regulations, as well as peer group rules and nuances of which behaviours and ways of being provide a passport to belonging, as opposed to threats of exclusion.

This blueprint ultimately defines a sense of self that carves up the unconscious potential of who a person could be to create a small arena of 'awareness' that a person believes is all of who they are. There is indeed wounding in the unconscious, but the biggest gift that Assagioli and Jung offer to us is that there is also potential, expansiveness, aliveness and connectedness to more than just the tribe in the unconscious of the psyche; therefore, expanding the field of awareness is what we are the most interested in as therapists. Because of course we are told we mustn't be too big, expansive, connected, joyful, excited, explorative, inspired, intuitive, wise, powerful, challenging or insightful by our families and communities, as well as being told we mustn't be too angry, outspoken, direct, argumentative, disagreeable, sad, or disappointed, to name but a few of the 'ways of being' that are disallowed, as we discover what our worlds will and won't accept as we grow up.

In order to ground these concepts and make them accessible to the client, it is useful to personify both Me and Not Me content into 'figures' that inhabit both our unconscious and conscious territory, once we begin to map a client's landscape. This means exploring 'who' within their psyche they identify as being, and who they do not. The 'Me' field of awareness denotes that which we are conscious of being, and the 'Not Me' field of unconsciousness describes that which we are not conscious of being. As we listen to clients, to their preferences, their beliefs about themselves and the world, the people they like and don't like, and the way they describe their school days, family of origin and friendship groups, we can begin to map the acceptable and the unacceptable.

It is often easiest when meeting a client to map 'Not Me' first, as it is the unacceptable that has become problematic when someone comes for therapy. Sometimes clients apologize for 'complaining' but it is this venting that allows the therapist to map 'Not Me' territory. Encouraging the client to tell their story in as much detail as possible is extremely useful to uncover the detail of who and what bothers them, as opposed to therapists jumping into wanting clients to feel and express more emotion in sessions, which, while useful as a longer term aim, is not so useful in terms of mapping process in order to get a sense of the client's landscape. Mapping in this way, rather than engaging in analytical assessments, avoids the pitfalls of therapists using psychobabble language that clients don't understand, instead utilizing the client's own language and everyday scenarios that make sense to them.

Mapping 'Not Me'

• What qualities, behaviours, self-expression, ways of being were disapproved of in the early parts of the client's life? This includes what was disapproved of in their family, school, religious organizations, work environments and friendship groups (adolescence and young adulthood is as important as early childhood). Those qualities can be put into the Not Me part of the map.

• Who do they disapprove of in their lives today? Who are they arguing with? What do they feel strong judgements about? What beliefs do they hold around right and wrong, good and bad?

• What feelings or behaviours would they rather not have?

• What parts of themselves or their lives would they like to get rid of? Those behaviours, feelings, impulses, sensations, longings, ideas and symptoms can be put into the Not Me part of the map.

Look at the qualities and behaviours in the Not Me territory and assume that the exact opposite of those qualities can be put in the Me part of the map.

Mapping 'Me'

Having mapped Not Me, you should already have some behaviour, feelings and qualities in the Me part of the map.

- What qualities, behaviours, self-expression, ways of being were approved of in the early parts of their lives? This includes what was approved of and rewarded in their family, school, religious organizations, work environments and friendship groups (adolescence and young adulthood is as important as early childhood). Those qualities can be put into the Me part of the map.

- Who do they approve of and admire in their lives today? Who would they like to be closer to? What belief do they hold around what is right in the world, how people should behave, what do they have a sense of justice around, who and what deserves love and support?

- If a client approves of and admires certain people and behaviour, but says they do not feel that they have those behaviours, you can put the behaviour they admire in the Not Me part of the map, and the opposite of it in the Me part of the map. These qualities are longed for parts buried in the unconscious that they do not yet feel able to take ownership of.

Look at the qualities and behaviours in the Me territory and assume that the exact opposite of those qualities belong in the Not Me territory.

The 'Edge' to the field of awareness

The city wall edge of awareness, or 'the Edge' between Me and Not Me territory, is the place where we can most effectively work as therapists with our clients. Rather than taking a torch and blundering into the dark woods of the unconscious landscape, all we need to do is to camp out at the edge of a client's conscious awareness and watch the unconscious, denied, disowned material emerging over the edge as troublesome symptoms. The unconscious is very much like the disgruntled, marginalized elements of a community that eventually becomes disturbed enough to attempt a revolution. Although our Edge defences are strong, we cannot keep unconscious material out forever. We do not need to go looking for the unconscious, it comes looking for us in the form of unconscious acting out – in symptoms such as depression, anxiety, malaise, relationship problems, work issues, health issues, parenting stress, and the many mood and personality disorders that bring clients into therapy.

As shown in Figure 7 below, I have further simplified the Field of Awareness map by zooming in on the edge around the Field of Awareness. On the map below, I have included some examples of the sorts of Not Me material that can bring clients into therapy and the equal and opposite Me material that sits in polarization to that Not Me material.

As you can see from the diagram, qualities and behaviours tend to become split and polarized both intra psychically and interpersonally, causing internal and external conflicts between ways of being that become competitors rather than mutually welcome, differentiated ways of being. This tendency to wage war, rather than integrate polarities, is one of the single most troublesome elements for psychotherapists to deal with and is very much evidenced in the way the world works, with countries waging war against each other and ideologies seeking to wipe each other out. Attempting to 'kill off' the parts of ourselves that we deem unacceptable makes therapy a dynamic and difficult space to work in, and yet, if we are to be relevant as therapists, we must engage with this continual background conflict, and learn to participate in a way that brings more capacity to mediate rather than to ally with one side of the conflict (the side we, as therapists, have a preference for).

Figure 7. Map of the Edge activity around the Field of Awareness.

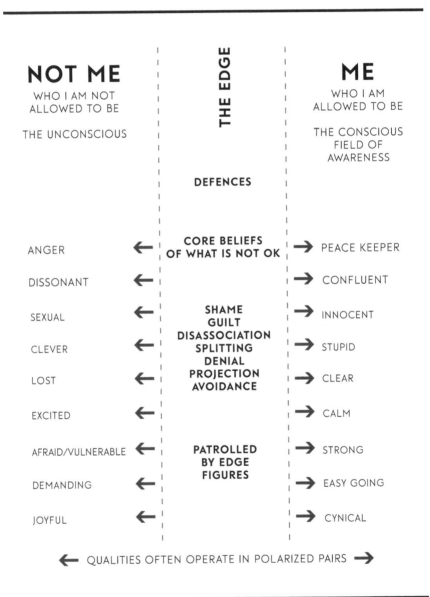

NOT ME	THE EDGE	ME
WHO I AM NOT ALLOWED TO BE		WHO I AM ALLOWED TO BE
THE UNCONSCIOUS		THE CONSCIOUS FIELD OF AWARENESS
	DEFENCES	
ANGER ←	CORE BELIEFS OF WHAT IS NOT OK	→ PEACE KEEPER
DISSONANT ←		→ CONFLUENT
SEXUAL ←	SHAME GUILT	→ INNOCENT
CLEVER ←	DISASSOCIATION SPLITTING	→ STUPID
LOST ←	DENIAL PROJECTION AVOIDANCE	→ CLEAR
EXCITED ←		→ CALM
AFRAID/VULNERABLE ←	PATROLLED BY EDGE FIGURES	→ STRONG
DEMANDING ←		→ EASY GOING
JOYFUL ←		→ CYNICAL

← QUALITIES OFTEN OPERATE IN POLARIZED PAIRS →

THE EDGE
STACEY MILLICHAMP

Edge figures

The most important elements to work with at this stage are the defences, core beliefs and psychopathology that define, protect and operate at the Edge. I use the term 'Edge figures' to personify this pathology, because along with the city wall that protects the status quo from the marginalized elements of the psyche, Edge figures operate very much like military police, armed and danger-ous, patrolling the Edge between the conscious and unconscious, and they can use similar intimidation tactics and threats to keep unconscious material at bay. Understanding these Edge defences, and learning to work with them more effectively, is one of the most useful ways to teach clients to become more skilled at facil-itating unconscious Not Me material over the Edge into aware-ness, rather than following the compulsion to shut the unconscious down. This leads to a better flow of unconscious con-tent, keeping the field of awareness irrigated with new ideas, ex-citing possibilities and sufficient challenge to feel more alive, as opposed to the aridness of a hermetically sealed off field of aware-ness where all unconscious content is kept out, leaving a flat, unin-spired and bleak sense of aliveness.

For clients who, because of the nature of their psychopathol-ogy, have too few Edge police patrolling the Edge between their conscious and unconscious territory – leading to an undifferenti-ated sense of self, fragmentation and psychotic episodes – the Edge needs to be built up, through teaching and facilitating firmer boundaries, a stronger sense of Me Identity, and more capacity to differentiate themselves from others. Working in the here and now with these clients is vitally important, utilizing the relational space where the experience of 'what is real' can be identified be-tween therapist and client. Creating a more resilient Edge around a client's field of awareness may entail skilling up their Edge fig-ures; teaching clients better discrimination, enabling them to look at the evidence of the here and now rather than allowing them to fanaticize about what may be real; helping them to practice get-ting reality checks in relation to other people; and practising with them to assert healthy boundaries rather than relying on subterranean methods for creating space (often through a push/pull dynamic with others).

As you can see from the previous diagram, Edge figures patrol the Edge between the unconscious Not Me territory and the conscious Me territory. In an ideal world, these figures create our defences against being overwhelmed with too much unconscious content, allowing us to maintain a sense of identity (Me), and giving us a sense of psychological cohesion.

Rigid Edge figures

In reality, Edge figures might police in too militant a way, creating a rigid wall around our field of awareness (Me) and cutting us off from the benefit of unconscious material. This is often a result of growing up in a rigid environment with very fixed ideas and beliefs of right and wrong, and this rigidity is internalized by the child so that the field of awareness is too impermeable, keeping out all unconscious content. This leads to very black and white thinking – 'I am right, and you are wrong' – in which all that are in the right should be protected and all that are in the wrong should be punished. This extreme black/white, right/wrong thinking leads to a lot of conflict in a person's internal and external world as they seek to fight the 'wrong' in themselves and others.

Extreme Edge figures

Conversely, extreme Edge figures can also occur if a child grows up in an environment where carers were incapacitated or absent, leaving the child to fend for themselves, generating pseudo-adult, two-dimensional superhero/villain Edge figures who rule with an iron fist. In this world, right and wrong, black and white are also extreme. The rules are strict and those who break them deserve punishment.

If you watch primary school children playing together there is often a 'Lord of the Flies' scenario set up where the goodies and the baddies are pitted against each other, punitive punishments are laid down, the baddies are slain and the good prevail. In the young psychological world of children, there is no middle ground of 'we are all full of goodies and baddies'; the immature psyche can only create splits between the acceptable and the unacceptable. Edge figures in these scenarios often show up as intrusive thoughts, obsessive compulsive symptoms, generalized anxiety, and personality disorders.

The intense internal worlds of children, run by the reptilian and limbic parts of the brain without the moderating insight of the prefrontal cortex (which doesn't finish developing into the early to mid-20's), will create allies and enemies. These parts of the brain control survival and emotion and will do whatever it takes to belong, fit in and stay alive in the tribe. It is the intervention of strong, empathic caretakers that activate and nourish the 'higher mind' prefrontal cortex, creating neural pathways of communication between the thinking/intuiting function of the frontal lobes and the survival and instinctive functions of the reptilian and limbic parts of the brain. Without those strong, empathic caretakers, a child will rely on their instinctive, survival self and fight to stay alive and to belong. This usually means slaying the enemy to their inherited beliefs, even if the enemy is within themselves, creating fierce battle lines between 'Me' and 'Not Me' that are as dangerous as the battle lines drawn between street gangs or wars fought between religions or countries.

Weak Edge figures

Conversely, we may not have strong enough Edge figures, because we have not been taught self-containment by caretakers who did not have cohesive identities and who lacked the strength themselves to model healthy boundaries. This lack of strong Edge figures, or good enough security guards at the gates to the city, means that there might be too much unconscious content flowing from the unconscious to the conscious field of awareness. 'Me' territory might be too fluid, never cohesive enough, leading to a fragmented sense of self, too much of a porous experience of the world and others, and a constant background anxiety from knowing that 'the door is always open and anyone can come on in'.

Edge figures are formed through the taboos of the community we grew up in, with inherited fears of the consequences if we cease to behave ourselves in the way that we have been taught we should. Those tribal taboos are utilized by Edge figures who use the weapons of shame and guilt attacks, threats of being annihilated, abandoned or ex-communicated, to keep unconscious material away from the city walls and the status quo of the field of awareness untouched. Edge figures might mimic the way in which caretakers and authority figures expressed themselves while we were young, and therefore they 'police' our Edges in a similar fashion to the ways in which our parents, teachers and peer group power dynamics kept order. This mimicking of 'how to keep order' is a key part of psychotherapy, as clients work with changing the 'internal world order' that they created as children.

How to work with Not Me material

This is where integrative work fully comes into its own, because as practitioners we need to be able to incorporate many different ways of unfolding unconscious process once we have developed some sense of the map we are working with, in collaboration with the client.

The 'Edgy material' from the unconscious is typically split off and repressed/suppressed, denied and projected onto or into (projective identification) others. Evacuating psychological content in this way is a common way of keeping unconscious material away from our conscious field of awareness, and is the cause of much of the conflict, misunderstanding and suffering in our world today. Whilst making all unacceptable behaviour acceptable is not the aim, developing a degree of understanding and familiarity with the primal unconscious material that drives much of the 'bad behaviour' in our world, is a way of developing more mastery, creating fewer polarizations with others, and limiting the amount of unconscious behaviour that we ourselves engage in.

How to facilitate Not Me material over the Edge into the field of awareness:

- Incorporate the client's Not Me material into our style as the therapist. For example:

  1 If setting boundaries and being clear is in the Not Me territory the therapist can model that way of being through the clarity of their own working conditions, being clear with the start and finish times of sessions, following through with cancellation fees, and being more direct with the client.

  2 If vulnerability and openness is in the Not Me territory for the client, the therapist can model openess and vulnerability in the consulting room, sharing more of what is meaningful for them, and talking about vulnerability in a way that honours qualities of kindness, receptivity, intuitive sensing and the ability to not know.

  3 If a client disowns being challenging in their lives or disagreeing with others, then use a more challenging style with the client, risk a conflict, as Not Me material is available in the field between therapist and client and can be welcomed in by either. If this leads to a conflict, and the client feels permission to lose their temper with you, or disagree back, you can debate this and thereby practice 'real life' embodiment of the quality and emotion of challenge. This makes the therapy room a much more real place, rather than a sanitized, protected bubble where clients are only ever made to feel safe, giving them no real-life practice of the very things they are struggling with.

- Utilize transference perspectives from the psychodynamic and psychoanalytic world. This means inquiring into the transference that your client may have towards you. It also means noticing your own countertransference thoughts, feelings, impulses, images, and sensations. Allow yourself to be a conduit for unconscious material in the room, and share your experience with the client, of what might be 'around' or emerging whilst you work. As a therapist, learning to describe your countertransference as a sense of what might be emerging between you and in a way that does not create blame – but rather brings a welcoming curiosity to what is being constellated – brings mutual engagement and aliveness to the therapeutic relationship.

- Use cognitive and mentalization approaches to identify the core beliefs underpinning the denial or rejection of certain ways of being/thinking/behaving and work together to challenge and soften those beliefs or to enlarge them to incorporate more acceptance of unconscious material. Mentalization is a very useful way to teach a client to slow things down and notice the triggering thoughts that lead to emotional decisions about reality, and to interrupt those habitual assumptions with the understanding that those are just ideas that the client holds about reality, and those ideas may not be true. Teaching clients to check out reality, rather than make assumptions about it from habitual thinking patterns, is an extremely important part of therapy.

- Use behavioural approaches that encourage the client to practice new ways of speaking, dressing, behaving and relating, that incorporate the denied within the unconscious. 'Acting as if' is a very useful way of trying out new (previously denied) ways of being; in the consulting room to start with, then in environments that feel safe enough to practice in. Thinking and feeling follows behaviour, just as much as behaviour follows thinking and feeling. Gestalt approaches that support clients to 'try on' the roles and figures within their unconscious territory in therapy, are very useful in the journey towards integrating those behaviours into their sense of identity.

- Use visualization techniques that support the client to imagine meeting the disowned figures within their unconscious. This may mean visualizing the young parts of themselves that have been pushed away, or it may mean visualizing and dialoguing with bullying, powerful, or sexual parts of themselves that have been denied (to name but a few). Visualization is very useful because it can facilitate personifying the elements in the unconscious which make them easier to grasp and work with for clients, and as dialogue is developed, relationships can be formed between the client's sense of identity and their unconscious figures (sub-personalities).

- Visualization may feel safer for a client who is not yet ready to engage in role-playing. Additionally, visualization can help a client to identify healthy caretaker figures internally, wise figures and other allies, to support them to cope with harsh Edge figures that are critical and shaming. Even warrior figures can be visualized to challenge Edge figure police to create a more even balance between strong elements in the psyche that can fight for the client's wellbeing.

- Use art therapy approaches through the use of drawing, clay modelling, collage work, and sand tray that encourage the client to image their unconscious material in a literal way that can be touched, felt and dialogued with.

- Use movement and dance therapy approaches that encourage the client to move as if they are the Not Me elements in their unconscious, bypassing the cognitive and allowing a more instinctive engagement with unconscious material.

- Use music therapy approaches through sounding out what is more primal and disavowed, or writing song lyrics and poetry that enables unconscious material to be expressed.

- Always incorporate a relational approach that accepts the possibility that unconscious field content can be experienced by the therapist as well as by the client. Any therapeutic approach is useful when unfolding unconscious material, as long as the therapist is incorporating a field perspective. This leads to a much more dynamic engagement where the therapist and client are both occupying and affecting the field of engagement that they are creating together, rather than the therapist being viewed as a neutral observer whose job it is to reflect what the client is bringing to the space.

If the therapist believes themselves to be sitting 'outside' the client's landscape, then splits will begin to occur between the therapist and client, with the client being seen as the one 'with the problem' who needs helping, and the therapist as the collected, neutral, one 'who knows'. This leads to the therapist disavowing much of the rich countertransference material that they may experience during the sessions, choosing instead to take such material to supervision where it is processed and brought back to the client in a sanitized way. Whilst it is certainly appropriate that therapists are cautioned against 'acting out' with clients, it is important for the sake of the therapist, the client and the relational field developing between them, that the therapist perceives themselves as part of the field at play with a client.

As unconscious Not Me content is unfolded and engaged with, it is important that the therapist encourages the client to come back to their Me territory, grounding what they have discovered and choosing which elements from their Not Me experiences they wish to practice including in their everyday way of being. This choosing is extremely important as we practice making conscious acts of will to move towards who we want to be in life, rather than feeling at the mercy of our own unconscious forces. This takes us on to a discussion of the role of the 'I' in psychosynthesis.

The function of the 'I'

Referring to Assagioli's egg diagram at the beginning of this chapter, Assagioli saw 'the conscious self, or the 'I', as being at the centre of the field of awareness, with an energetic and intuitive connection to 'the higher self.'

Assagioli described the conscious self or 'I' as

> ... the point of pure self-awareness, often confused with the conscious personality just described (the field of conscious awareness), but in reality, it is quite different from it. This can be ascertained by the careful use of introspection. The changing contents of our consciousness (the sensations, thoughts, feelings, etc.) are one thing, while the 'I', the self, the centre of our consciousness is another. From a certain point of view this difference can be compared to that existing between the white lighted area on a screen and the various pictures which are projected upon it.[3]

When training students, I often find a lot of vague generalizations expressed about these more abstract elements of psychosynthesis, and concepts of the 'I' seem to invite the most confusion. Therefore, it is important to seek grounded specificity within these concepts. The 'I' can be viewed as a satellite of awareness that is able to move around the landscape of the psyche. It is the 'I am-ness' that creates a sense of beingness. Beyond our identity of who we think we are, therefore beyond the content of our field of awareness, lays the vast unconscious territory of Not Me. The 'I' within each of us operates as an emissary of the Universal Self (as discussed in Chapter 2, that part of the psyche that is in touch with the collective field, as well as the personal field). The 'I' can identify with sub-personalities, or complexes inside of us, experience the unconscious elements that are emerging over the Edge into our awareness, and then dis-identify from those elements, creating a sense of 'I am this too'.

The 'I' as a satellite of awareness that can move around in our internal landscapes creates a witnessing and describing meta-communicating capacity which can experience unconscious personal and collective fields. This contactful inquiry creates connections that mimic neural pathways connecting to the many different parts within us and between us. As we journey beyond our familiar ground, we move out of being possessed or trapped in a sense of identifying only with the Me territory of the conscious field of awareness. The more we burn the wood of our personal identity the more we realize that we are not just the Me that we thought we were; our field of awareness is largely full of preferences rather than 'who I really am' and there is a large amount of unconscious material that is unexplored.

As we come to realize that we are much more complex than previously assumed, we can become more fluid travellers within our own psyches, capable of engaging with, experiencing and liberating lost parts of ourselves, and discovering the transpersonal qualities buried within the complexes and subpersonalities that inhabit our unconscious. These transpersonal qualities often have archetypal blueprints that charge our unconscious material with collective patterns of being, and the 'I' has the capacity to identify with and unfold this material, potentially connecting us to a sense of being part of humanity beyond cultural and geographical differences.

How to develop the 'I'

The 'I' is therefore the most essential part of ourselves, and the most essential part of being a good therapist. When we develop our awareness as a tool for witnessing, encountering, exploring, and inquiring into our own thoughts, feelings, assumptions, sensations, and meaning making, then we are strengthening the 'I'. The same is true when we develop our capacity to focus on the client's meaning making; especially the sub-text behind someone's words, noticing the small signals that they give off, and the atmosphere that is generated as they speak. The 'I' has an ability to notice internal experience while external content is being shared by the client. The 'I' has the capacity to notice primary content being expressed, whilst also noticing secondary, 'background' signals.

Developing the 'I' is much like building a muscle, the more we learn to create a focus that is both alert, yet also relaxed, the stronger our capacity as therapists becomes to follow the client's content, whilst picking up the subtle themes and areas that are the most charged with importance. Many of the great spiritual traditions are fundamentally teaching students to develop their 'I' through meditative practices, which involves the practice of alert focus, whilst noticing transient thoughts, feelings and sensations that are observed but allowed to pass.

Psychosynthesis encourages the identification with and inquiry into cognitive and experiential states to further unfold them, and then to dis-identify from those states to continue exploring what else might be present. The very process of dis-identifying from a way of thinking and feeling reminds us that this is an idea, sensation or feeling that we are having, which has its own relevance, but that we are fundamentally more than that these ideas, sensations and feelings.

Assagioli wrote that 'we are dominated by everything with which our self becomes identified. We can dominate and control everything from which we dis-identify ourselves'.[4] Whilst I'm not sure I agree that we can control everything from which we dis-identify, I certainly have experienced and witnessed the process of identification with unconscious material, and then the process of dis-identifying from it, which creates more of a sense of self-mastery whereby the powerful primitive haunting from disowned unconscious material becomes more contained within our conscious awareness and capacity to harness it.

Perhaps therapy is a form of conflict resolution between Me and Not Me material, mediated by the 'I' as a satellite of awareness. Mediation allows a brokering of deals that provide space and value for both the conscious and the unconscious, rather than allowing on-going warfare within the psyche, which is often played out in the relationships that people have with those around them.

Useful tools for developing connection with the 'I' point of awareness

- Develop a narrating voice internally that notices and describes what is occurring internally and externally. This feels like an internal storyteller, which has a meta-communicating function, noticing the micro without preferences or judgement, simply describing it to you. This might be described as 'talking to yourself' but in reality it is the development of an internal narrator who is practising focused awareness and picking up on details without analysis.

- Any meditative and mindfulness practices strengthen connection to the 'I', because during these practices we are learning to silence much of the monkey mind chatter, making it easier to observe and notice, rather than being lost in our internal content. Moving meditation can also be important; some people find certain dance practises, yoga practices and exercises such as running and even walking, also give them the ability to move beyond the everyday chatter in their minds to a deeper sense of connection with a witnessing silence.

- Choosing to say 'yes' to internal experiences that are uncomfortable, rather than pushing them away; bringing an attitude of inquiry to those experiences and choosing to move towards what is uncomfortable and suspending assumptions that something is wrong, which can generate premature closure to processes. Cultivating an attitude of patience towards experience and suspending 'right/wrong' thinking means suspending the assumption that we know what is going on; and learning to pick up a trail that we can gently hunt by following the scent and paper trail, assuming that it will take us somewhere useful.

- Respecting the unconscious as a vast and unknown landscape that requires patience and regard as we inquire into it. This develops the humility of knowing that we have only a small amount of understanding of our own and others' psyches and that the hunting capacity of the 'I', which is alert to the subtle in ourselves and others, is the most useful place from which to practice our inquiry.

[1] D. Shultz and S. Shultz, *Theories of Personality*, 9th edn (Belmont, CA: Wadsworth, Cengage Learning, 2009).

[2] Diana Whitmore, *Psychosynthesis Counselling in action* (London: Sage Publications Ltd., 2014), p. 86.

[3] Roberto Assagioli, *Psychosynthesis* (London: Thorsons, 1965), p. 18.

[4] Roberto Assagioli, *Psychosynthesis*, p. 22.

Chapter 4

The Walled Garden of the Psyche

Working at depth

What does 'working at depth' mean in our therapeutic work? Does one therapeutic approach work more 'at depth' than another? These are questions that are often raised in trainings by students who are rightly seeking to make sense of such concepts when faced with the reality of their clinical work with clients. In response to these questions, I have developed a model that I call 'the walled garden of the psyche', which I offer as a suggested map for how to work at depth with clients within an integrative framework. Students are often confused by how psychodynamic, existential, psychoanalytic, and transpersonal approaches interface within client work, as they are usually taught as separate modules within a training programme, with insufficient attention given to the ways in which these approaches overlap. Additionally, there can be confusion about how these different schools of thought can be applied in short-term contracts with clients, as well as in longer-term work.

Short-term vs long-term therapy

A client's therapeutic journey may be short term or it may be a longer exploration through several psychological landscapes, with adventures, dragons to be slain, parts of the self to be discovered and rescued from imprisonment, and daemon allies to be met and partnered with. In the past, many psychotherapy trainings defined depth work as relating to the length of time that a client stayed in therapy, with the assumption that the longer the period of therapy, the deeper the client could go. However, practitioners are now required to respond to a changing economic climate which often calls for short-term work, with measurable outcomes utilized to justify funding streams, and private practice clients expecting change in a short space of time. Therefore, it is important to address how to work at depth within short-term therapeutic work, as well as longer-term work.

Whilst it is true that a long-term, resilient and trusted therapeutic relationship allows deep work to unfold, it is not necessarily the case that short-term work, in contrast, is shallow, purely solution focused or without depth of connection and mutual meaning making in relation to presenting issues. If we map how the client is relating in the here and now, through observing their use of language, the core beliefs that construct their reality, and the way in which they set up the relational space with us as therapists, then we are already working at depth in terms of how the client structures (and therefore experiences) reality.

The idea that depth can only be found by de-constructing a client's autobiographical past is not the whole truth; childhood experiences do indeed create blueprints for clients that define their unconscious/conscious territories and uncovering those blueprints to make sense of the way in which they construct reality today, in the here and now, is extremely useful. However, even within short-term therapy we can find out a lot about a client's meaning making process and help them to practice exploring new territory, without having to always understand why a client has fenced off that territory as disallowed.

Unexplored psychological territory and disallowed ways of being carry some shame, guilt and fear, and a trusted therapeutic relationship can support a client to allow themselves to go over edges into the unknown. It might also be the case that clients become too comfortable and familiar with a therapist in a long-term relationship if both go to sleep in some way. Far from the attachment between the two enabling deep work, sometimes it can create mutual edges beyond which the work never goes.

Working at depth is achieved through the presence and focus of the therapist, their willingness to challenge themselves in relationship to their own edges, and their openness to being dynamically engaged with the client. This is not related to the length of time spent working with a client, instead it relates to the therapist's way of being with them. This entails a therapist having a broad bandwidth of personal experience with entering the unfamiliar in their own experience, challenging themselves, and learning to move towards, rather than away from, what feels unknown and sometimes frightening. Having strengthened their own ability to journey psychologically, a therapist is better equipped to function as a valid guide and companion, capable of relating to what is emerging for the client and within the field of the relationship at any given moment.

The walled garden

Through teaching modules on how to work at depth as a psychotherapist, I have developed a model which I call 'the walled garden of the psyche', intended as a simple map for the many different levels and layers to the here and now of the therapeutic journey. From a field theory perspective, working at depth is not a linear road where the work deepens to new layers the longer the client stays. It can certainly be true that there is a natural progression from the outside layers to more core material; however, I have depicted the different layers of work as a field of influence in order to support practitioners to get a better handle on the different theoretical models that are relevant at various stages within client work. Rather than progressing smoothly through each layer, we often find ourselves only working in one layer with a client, or find ourselves jumping into new layers without warning. The diagram is therefore a depiction of the field at any one time, and we must trust ourselves to stay true to what is emerging and learn to follow it, no matter how idiosyncratic the dynamic!

Developing descriptive language

Some counselling and psychotherapy trainings seem to have drifted toward a general belief that feelings and emotions are more important than thoughts; this creates an edge which favours ex-

Figure 8. The Walled Garden of the Psyche.

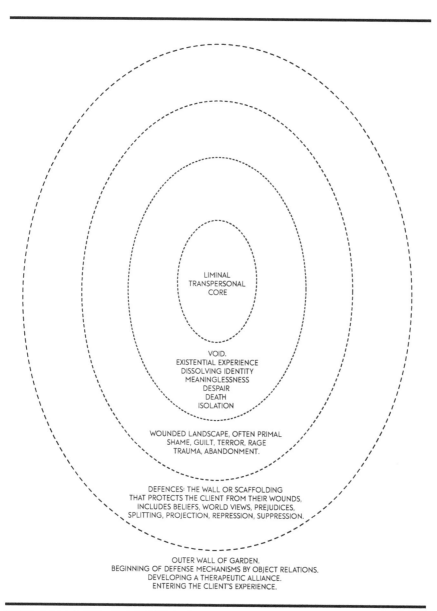

LIMINAL
TRANSPERSONAL
CORE

VOID.
EXISTENTIAL EXPERIENCE
DISSOLVING IDENTITY
MEANINGLESSNESS
DESPAIR
DEATH
ISOLATION

WOUNDED LANDSCAPE, OFTEN PRIMAL
SHAME, GUILT, TERROR, RAGE
TRAUMA, ABANDONMENT.

DEFENCES: THE WALL OR SCAFFOLDING
THAT PROTECTS THE CLIENT FROM THEIR WOUNDS,
INCLUDES BELIEFS, WORLD VIEWS, PREJUDICES,
SPLITTING, PROJECTION, REPRESSION, SUPPRESSION.

OUTER WALL OF GARDEN.
BEGINNING OF DEFENSE MECHANISMS BY OBJECT RELATIONS.
DEVELOPING A THERAPEUTIC ALLIANCE.
ENTERING THE CLIENT'S EXPERIENCE.

THE WALLED GARDEN OF THE PSYCHE
STACEY MILLICHAMP

periencing rather than thinking about experience. The point is to be able to do both, and the walled garden map incorporates the different relational and meaning making territory that we may find ourselves in with clients, with each having a specific focus, task and purpose.

Identifying which part of the field landscape we are in, at any given moment, enables us as therapists to describe to the client what is occurring in the work. As a talking approach, we need to fill our libraries with a broad range of vocabulary, metaphors, symbols and images drawn from both ancient models and current cultural references such as political and world events, films, books, television programmes, scientific and digital developments, music, poetry, art and dance. We are constantly surrounded by metaphorical material which we can use to put words and concepts to the relational, existential and transpersonal landscapes that we are in with our clients.

Words and ideas can be catalytic if we practice using them to paint landscapes that make sense to our clients, rather than using psychological theoretical language which might make sense to the therapeutically trained, but not to the clients that we are working with. It is also the case that as therapists we have come to assume that we understand what we mean by such theories as transference and countertransference, existential material, attachment styles, object relations and so on. However, when asked to explain what we understand by these concepts, many therapists will admit that they neither fully grasp what such terms really mean nor how they apply to the reality of what is occurring with their clients. It is therefore vital that we strengthen our verbal and conceptual musculature through finding different ways of describing the same phenomena, using everyday language that makes sense to us and to our clients.

The walled garden as metaphor

So, let us look at the walled garden as another way to describe the story of what is occurring with our clients, without attachment to processes unfolding in a linear way where we simply progress from one layer to another in an orderly fashion, but rather as different parts of the field landscape that we are inhabiting at any one time. This model is not in any way an exhaustive exploration of the different issues that we face as therapists, and each training model has its own way of working with the themes outlined here; this material is intended as an outline to give us a starting point as therapists when we find ourselves asking 'where are we now?'

I have used a walled garden as a metaphor for psychological landscape because it creates a sense of containment for what can otherwise feel like a galaxy of unconscious material. The model is offered as a structure for defining the layers that we might work with as therapists and aims to de-bunk the idea that the more existential and transpersonal the client material gets, the more 'out there' it gets. Instead, the model utilizes the felt sense of getting deeper into 'the heart of the matter' or deeper into 'the core of things'.

Much like the walled city metaphor used in previous chapters, there is a level of permission granted by a client as they let us, as practitioners, into more unknown and unconscious arenas and the boundary edges that demarcate the moving from one layer or way of being to another, is of vital importance. Working at an edge that defines a shift in landscape is important to identify and describe, as it helps the client to understand feelings and thoughts that might seem unusual to them. Learning to map psychological landscape, and to notice when they are moving over edges within that landscape, helps clients to have more of a sense of mastery over 'where they are' in their lives, and to utilize the different attitudes, behaviour and self-support that most benefits what they need at any given time.

When reading the definitions of each layer of the walled garden, please do remember that this is a metaphorical way of looking at the different stages of therapy, and it is not therefore intended as a concrete, literal way of looking at a linear development of the therapeutic relationship.

The outer wall of the garden

The outer wall of the garden (psyche) is where we spend a lot of time when we first meet, assess, and begin our therapeutic journey with a client. It might also be where we find ourselves after a rupture with a client, when we are nearing a conflict having unintentionally contravened a hidden code of conduct that the client holds dear, when we have stumbled across wounded territory that we didn't know was there, or when intense transference is stirred up in the relationship. Life events can also put us back outside the garden facing the outermost wall, such as the client experiencing a trauma, losing a job or significant relationship, or in any way unexpectedly having the rug pulled out from under them. At times, it can feel as if we are almost 'starting again'.

The outer wall presents us with the client's 'front of house', much like walking into a restaurant and being greeted by the headwaiter, with no sense of what is happening behind the scenes in the kitchen and staff room. This front of house, or face to the world, is where we find 'Me' territory (in reference to our mapping of clients from Chapter 3). The client's front of house includes their manner, tone of voice, how they dress, the way they describe themselves, whether they are confluent or dissonant in how they establish contact with us –and therefore whether they would like to create mutual ground off the bat – or whether they would like to make it clear that they are different from us with more debate and disagreement from the get-go. This arena tells us a lot about the client's survival strategy and who they think they must be in order to maintain liberty, whilst also being accepted.

Relations and attachment preferences

This territory is therefore mediated by the client's object relations and attachment preferences. There are many good books written on the psychodynamic theory of object relations and attachment structures, which the reader can explore in-depth. Here, as we are using layman's language for psychological terms which can be shared with clients to describe and build conceptual bridges for them, let us think about these perspectives in ordinary terminology. People that matter to us when we are growing up, as well as when we are adults, are internalized in a very important way. Those people's way of being and their way of relating are ingested by us – or in quantum terms as outlined in Chapter 2, their wave patterns are laid down in some essential way within us – so that they become part of who we are, how we perceive the world, relate, and behave.

That does not stop once we have grown up. As we continue to form relationships and attachments to friends, partners, colleagues, peers, children and family, we are in a constant state of letting others in and re-forming ourselves in order to incorporate new ways of responding to the world that is also changing around us. This internalizing mostly happens on an unconscious level, and it is useful to create feedback loops with clients that describe how it is to relate to them, as this is feedback that the world hardly ever gives people in a compassionate way, making it difficult for them to understand how they come across to others.

Describing and discussing with clients how they like to set up the relational space is an important task that can take up the entirety of a short-term piece of work. This is especially the case if a client presents with relational problems, conflict at work, a desire to meet a partner, problems with friends, or indeed any issue that involves them setting up good relationships with others. Whilst longer-term work can help a client to delve more deeply into why they relate in the way that they do, or how their front of house came to be the way it is, it is not essential to do that autobiographical excavation in order to identify their current way of relating and practising making helpful changes, if the client only has a short term, time limited contract with a therapist.

Early dialogues with clients

Working with a client's way of attaching is a slightly different matter. Although it is possible to map and describe how the client initially forms an attachment to you as their therapist, in short-term work there isn't necessarily the same investment that goes into their longer-term relationships and therefore the experience of a long term commitment, and the level of comfort or discomfort that comes with that, is hard to replicate in short-term therapy.

Some people find the beginning of relationships much more comfortable, with a well-constructed front of house, finding mutual ground easily and coming across as confident and at ease. Of course, this in and of itself is interesting to observe if the client has come with a presenting issue regarding relationships. Describing how it is to meet and be with a client in the first few sessions, and working on our ability to articulate what we observe, helps to set up the therapeutic alliance and gives the client feedback to chew on and begin to assimilate. Clients might reject our observations, take offence, and seek to correct us; this is all useful grist for the mill in terms of finding out how clients identify themselves and whether our experience of them early on concurs or differs with their perceived image of themselves.

These early dialogues also create the basis for a relationship where there is permission to have debate and disagreement as well as agreement and mutual understanding. Starting as we mean to go on as therapists is important because we, too, are showing clients our front of house: the way in which we greet, open the space, and get to know our clients tell them a lot about who we are without us having to self-disclose information about our own lives. It also means that we are offering a relationship which holds some 'real world' practising of being more direct, authentic and trustworthy, because we are not keeping our observations to ourselves as therapists. Instead, we are creating a more democratic way of working by bringing a willingness to be thoughtfully transparent in the relational space, even if that causes waves.

Front of house examples

For example, a client may come into early sessions the same way each time; their posture might be burdened, they may avoid eye contact, make deep sighs, tell us how tired they are and warn us not to make them work too hard or to challenge them too much. This is sometimes the case with people who want us to be gentle with them, who have been quite bruised by life, and are seeking to express their vulnerability but do not feel safe enough to do so directly.

It can conversely be the case that individuals do not realize that they are indirectly asking us to be careful with them and to back off, when this type of presentation may come from a client who in fact wishes to have more robust contact, and who is coming to therapy to learn to handle conflict. In this case the front of house is a learned or inherited behaviour that goes against the authentic desire for relating with more traction and intensity. If we do not describe to them that their way of setting up contact is asking us to be careful, they may unconsciously create a gentle contact that they do not actually want, which will cause conflict with us later on down the line when they tell us that therapy isn't helping them because they have been treated with kid gloves!

A different example is a client who comes into early therapy with a bouncy greeting, a good sense of humour and an entertaining way of engaging you as their therapist. With clients like this it can be difficult to get a sense of why they are there, as their front of house is inviting, puts others at ease, and creates a stimulating atmosphere. These clients may come because they are the ones that others turn to when they need support, understanding and cheering up. Such clients may feel burned out and tired of being other people's go-to and need to explore alternative ways of being that express more of their own needs. Their 'not me' unconscious territory may be calling them to become more self-oriented for a while, even entering a more introverted period where their front of house extroverted ease with others takes a back seat and allows them to let go of the impulse to light up the room for others.

Conversely this type of front of house may camouflage a more aggressive presentation, the sense of humour bordering on the sarcastic and the extroversion throwing down a gauntlet of 'I don't need you, so what do you have to offer me?' A fear of being vulnerable, not being the one in charge in the room, a cynical fear that therapy won't help – or even that it might – can lie behind this way of engaging contact. Being robust enough as a therapist to experience, notice, and describe the way in which this client makes contact is vital if they are to take you seriously as someone who isn't afraid of them, but is instead interested in who they are and what they are needing, even if they spend most of the first few sessions explaining why they think it's impossible to get anything from you or anybody else.

The outer wall of the garden is not about finding solutions for clients or resolving the dilemmas and conflicts that they bring to therapy, it is about experiencing how they make contact, how they set up relationships, and how they generate intimacy (or not) in a way that begins to build a bridge of communication not just from client to therapist (the therapist passively receiving) but also from therapist to client (the therapist experiencing, observing, and sharing how it is to sit with and relate to the client.) In this way a dynamic exchange is set up and charges the relational space with the possibility of moving past the outer wall of the garden into the next layer, which is the landscape of the client's defences and their protective psychopathology.

Defences: the scaffolding which protects wounded territory

Once someone has presented their front of house sufficiently for the therapist to be considered safe and worthy of finding out more, there is usually either a disclosure from the client as to why they continue to have the problems that they are bringing to us, or they act out in some way to show us how they have created situations that don't work for them. At this stage it is important to remember that, while people can seem quite knowledgeable about themselves, they wouldn't be in therapy if they understood the whole story. For that reason, what somebody tells a therapist about themselves and why they think they have the problems that they have, is not as important as watching what they do in the therapy room, and especially by asking them to **describe** events in their everyday lives, instead of accepting their analysis of those events.

Therapists in particular can be very difficult clients, because the more versed we are in psychological terminology, the more analytical we may become and the less able we are to simply describe the nuts and bolts of our everyday story and to be transparent. What is commonly seen as psychological mindedness within the psychotherapy profession can be articulate defensiveness that makes it especially challenging to work beyond the front of house to deeper structures that are seeking expression through the presenting issues that bring someone to therapy.

Taboo territory

At each stage, as the client allows us across a boundary into deeper territory, there can be a strained moment in the therapy. There are many reasons for this, the primary one being that allowing another human being to see and experience the private (even from themselves) territory that they have fenced off and relegated to their unconscious territory is a strain that can bring conflicted feelings of 'I want to, but I also don't want to' and fears that they will be judged, or in some way rejected or taken advantage of, if they share taboo territory with another. As a therapist, it is important to expect that there will be moments of heightened tension with clients, sometimes out of the blue. They might express that it's time to leave therapy, that they feel better and don't need therapy anymore, or they don't feel better and think therapy is a waste of time.

Either way, whilst it may look as if this is a rupture in the relationship, often it is instead a signal that a client is getting ready to jump over an edge and take the therapist with them. As in a relationship where someone threatens to leave, to find out if their partner wants them to stay, it is a way of trying to elicit the therapist's real thoughts and feelings towards the client, and therefore whether it's safe to risk increased intimacy. This is a tricky time as therapists do not wish to be coercive with their clients. However, it is worth therapists presenting the choices available to the client, outlining that it may be a time to take a break and leave therapy as the initial presenting issue has quietened down, or conversely that they can stay and find out what is constellating for them in more unconscious ways.

Clients are often afraid that they are being self-indulgent or fear that either their problems are too big for therapists to handle or too small to matter. At this stage of the work it is important for the client to hear from their therapist that their experiences matter, that their conflicts have significance, and that they have co-created a therapeutic relationship that can be utilized for them to venture more deeply into themselves if they wish to, and that if they do, that their therapist will be right by their side.

The intelligence within defences

Sometimes it is the very way that the therapist responds to this prickly, sticky part of a client's landscape that is the medicine. This defended territory is protecting the next wounded layer of the walled garden, and the client needs to know that the therapist is respectful but also skilful in surviving this part of being with them. Being accepted for our front of house is not as important as being accepted in our defences, primarily because our front of house is more familiar to us and is by its very definition the face we have chosen to show the world.

Defensive territory is what we choose to hide, because we don't like our own wounded landscape and neither do we think others will like it, so we protect it with barbed wire, guard dogs, soldiers with weapons, or cloaks of invisibility. Referring back to the Edge figures described in Chapter 3, this is the part of the landscape that they are most active in; the biggest edges often border our wounded territory and what is buried there often contains our deepest longings and most painful disappointments, betrayals and lost innocence.

Therapists rightly tread carefully here, but it is important not to be so careful that we tiptoe around defences rather than encountering and naming them as worthy gate keepers that have kept a client safe and as sane as possible throughout their lives. In other words, these defensive structures are needed, although some of them may have outlived their usefulness and need to be reconfigured in some way.

There is an intelligence at work within our defences and it is important that that is honoured and neither ignored nor brushed past. Understanding the way our defences operate is gold dust and very few people will be willing or able to engage with us in figuring out how our unique configuration works. A good therapist will compassionately engage in helping to describe the nuts and bolts of how we have learned to keep ourselves protected without an agenda to change that; consequently, spending time in this part of the walled garden is vitally important if we are going to experience the primal, existential and transpersonal layers that are more deeply hidden.

Defence structure descriptions

Some of the best-known defence descriptions for the structures to be found here are denial, splitting, projective identification, projection, repression, suppression, sublimation and displacement. A client might be very fragmented and permeable, without access to a stable sense of self. Conversely a client may be very tightly bound together and impermeable, letting very little in and very little out. All of us are on a continuum somewhere on this spectrum. The Diagnostic and Statistical Manual of Mental Disorders (DSM-V) outlines in depth the clustering together of sets of symptoms that give us a way to describe the defensive psychopathology that clients bring to therapy.[1] If these descriptions are utilized with an understanding that our pathology is needed by us in this challenging world that we live in, that without it we would be overwhelmed by internal experiences and external events, then naming pathology in this way is useful rather than reductive.

As we seek to find language that we can use with clients that is understandable, it is essential as therapists to continue to utilize the feedback loops that we have created to describe our encounter with their defences. Very simply put, what most defences have in common is that there are ways of being that I have unconsciously deemed to be unacceptable and which have therefore been **denied, split off and**:

- Suppressed or repressed (buried) in my unconscious.

- Projected onto others, by assuming that *they* have those behaviours and ways of being, and denying that I myself have those thoughts, feelings and ways of being.

- Projected into others (projective identification). This is a more intense version of projection, where my split off, unwanted parts (part objects) – which can be loving as well as hateful – are evoked in another person through the way that I behave towards them. This occurs when I act towards someone else, such as my therapist, as if they are that unwanted part of me, with such intensity as to actually evoke those feelings and responses in that person. Field theory would suggest that disowned parts, and ways of being, operate as roles in the field which anyone can identify with, as we all share similar edges and experiences as human beings.

- Displaced onto other activities, things or people in a way that is less harmful to my way of life, such as shouting at other drivers whilst driving, when I am actually angry with my boss; or sublimated into more constructive activities, such as going to a boxing class when I am angry.

These defence structures share a hostile attitude towards certain ways of being, leading to denial of them, splitting them off, and putting them 'somewhere away from my sense of identity' and onto or into other people or activities. The me/not me edge work in the last chapter is a simple way of thinking about and talking about this part of a client's psyche; the way in which their landscape is guarded. By listening to ways of being and doing that they disown, judge, and deny having – and conversely the ways of being and doing that they admire, envy, long for, but deny having themselves – we can, as therapists, map what is allowed and disallowed, what is owned and what is denied, what is 'me' and what is 'not me'.

It is important to emphasize that what we deny and split off are not just primitive qualities such as hate, envy, rage, jealousy, greed, lust, dominance, etc., but also transpersonal qualities such as power, joy, love, bliss, inspiration, service, etc. We are often told as children not to be too much of anything, and that can include the bigness of our capacity and giftedness as well as the bigness of our primitive feelings. Oftentimes people are told that to fit in they need to conform to the middle ground of behaviour, and so they mute the intensity of themselves which might make them stand out. Conversely, they might keep an intensity of one end of the spectrum or the other and bury the opposite polarity.

Coming alive more fully in therapy involves expanding into that which is denied as 'not me', with an ally that we trust to go at a pace that we can handle and who has the capacity to name and therefore anchor the lost parts of us that are seeking expression by causing trouble with the status quo of our lives. Hearing a therapist say 'it seems as if you've decided that way of being and behaving is unacceptable; tell me how you see that as wrong...' allows us to start activating the next layer of the psyche, which is wounded territory.

Wounded territory

Once we have accurately described the ways in which a client has learned to keep themselves protected, we naturally start to activate the wounds that necessitated the construction of those defences. If we respectfully acknowledge those defences and seek to understand them without threatening them, then we may be given access to this wounded landscape.

These wounds might be generally from our family, school, religion, work, or peer tribes that explicitly or implicitly told us who we have to be in order to belong, to be loved, to have a roof over our heads and a place at the table of significance with those we love and admire.

This general wounding might not leave the ragged scars of the specific wounding from abuse or neglect, but it is an apportioning up of who we believe we can be and who we believe we cannot be, that everyone experiences to varying degrees.

If someone says 'I had a happy childhood', that may be true in terms of their overall experience of being loved, safe and encouraged, but there will always have been a degree of psychological marginalizing that occurs during formative years because it is a necessity in creating a civilized society or community that adheres to a set of rules, whether that is the rule of law, rule of education, rule of religion, rule of the family, or rule of the peer group that a person identifies with and wishes to be a part of. This includes gangs and any group that a person utilizes as a surrogate family or community that they must fit in with. Therefore, there is always a conscious, constructed sense of identity (who I am) and unconscious (who I am not) territory with edges that are defined by defences and core beliefs about what is and what is not ok.

Understanding our edges and going through the process of assessing how our unconscious is interfacing with our field of awareness means that we can relate with more awareness and take more responsibility for ourselves and the world around us. Therefore, excavating wounded territory is not just the work of cathartic uncovering, it is part of an on-going honest search for the truth of 'who we are' and that which connects us to the human experience in general.

Excavation

Excavation, as if on an archaeological dig, is a good description of this part of the walled garden. During the 1970s there was an explosion in the human potential movement with such movements as Primal Therapy developed by Arthur Janov, Encounter Groups, Rebirthing developed by Leonard Orr, Bioenergetics created by Alexander Lowen and contributions from many body psychotherapy approaches originating with William Reich. These therapies created therapeutic environments in which childhood trauma and other repressed experiences could be re-encountered and thereby 'released', often in a cathartic way. The concept of surfacing and experiencing primal material so that we might no longer be possessed by it was an important part of the humanistic movement and cathartic ways of working are still practiced by many therapists.

However, our developing understanding of the way in which the human brain works, helped by technological advances in brain scanning, means that neuroscience has had a big impact on the way we work with wounding and trauma. We now understand that wounds are not just cellular-level packages of pain that can be released or evacuated and then are magically gone. Our experiences as we grow and develop are mapped within us neurologically, with repeated experience and belief systems digging the deepest neural pathways in our brains. Like the chain gang, our experiences dig meaning making roads down which our experience travels, defining our sense of reality.

Our increased neurological understanding means that approaches such as EMDR (eye movement desensitization and reprocessing) can make an immediate difference to a client who is struggling with PTSD (post-traumatic stress disorder), and cognitive behavioural techniques such as mindfulness and mentalization are enabling practitioners to give clients tools that they themselves can use to feel more in charge of their inner worlds. With apps that can be downloaded and meditation now on the increase in the general population of the West, the public now wish to have more access to their own lifestyle changes and choices. In turn, this desire to be more self-defining and self-healing requires that we as practitioners view our therapeutic relationships as co-creative and collaborative, with psycho-education playing an important role in the therapeutic consulting room.

At a time when social media dominates the lives of many adults and young people and relationships are being sought on websites, a crisis of identity leading to resultant anxiety disorders and depression is a foreground issue for most practitioners. It is no longer sufficient to simply uncover trauma and wounding to allow repressed and suppressed parts of the unconscious to emerge. Clients are seeking to know themselves and to have better understanding and mastery over their own psyches.

Developing internal leadership

Transpersonal approaches have a lot to offer clients in terms of developing an internal leadership that draws on compassionate wisdom, from which to rule their inner kingdoms. Developing this internal leadership enables work in wounded territory to be a home coming if we encourage clients to approach this part of their internal worlds with respect, curiosity and an understanding that 'this story is mine and has gifts, as well as challenges for me'.

Enlarging a sense of personal story, of 'I am this too', with a clearer and expanded sense of identity, is the main purpose of working with wounded territory. Understanding the purpose of excavating here is vital if practitioners are going to work at depth, with wounding, in a useful way.

As a result, it is wise to metaphorically 'pitch a tent' at the edge of a client's wounded territory and wait to see what emerges. As therapeutic archaeologists we are interested in the bones of what is buried, to unearth fragments that slowly create a picture of the story within that landscape. Stories have key relationships, activities, tasks, loves, losses, hopes, dreams and pain. These stories are often spontaneously told to us by clients once we have explored the defences that keep them safe. Such stories can come through as night dreams, day dreams, spontaneous memories, a desire to talk to family members about family history, an interest in ancestry or a current life situation that sets off meaningful memories and a red thread of significance in a particular story of 'who I have had to be' or 'who I wanted to be'.

Parts of the psyche that have been dropped, left behind, segregated, or simply forgotten, can come through these stories within therapy as we seek to put the bones together and build a picture of the meaning within a client's life. This sense of story, which connects the different (often fragmented) parts of ourselves that matter the most, helps to create a coherent and coagulated sense of 'me-ness' that enables us to feel more solid, grounded, and intentional in ourselves and in the world.

Wounds are painful precisely because they point to something that matters deeply. This means that the stories of what mattered – but were lost, betrayed, discarded or forgotten – help us to recover what is essentially meaningful to us and to irrigate and replenish our field of awareness and sense of identity with a richer, more vibrant connection to deeper parts of who we are and who we wish to become. It can also mean challenging archaic or outmoded, inherited rules and roles that no longer apply, through re-negotiation with the Edge figures and core beliefs that have defined 'me' and 'not me' territory. Periods of therapeutic change that enable clients to enlarge their conscious awareness of themselves, through journeying to the archaeological landscape of their psyche and relating to what is emerging, means teaching them to relate in a new way.

Internal leadership is often defined and learned via important authority figures and caretakers in our lives. This can include political figures, being shaped by prevailing educational and religious norms, whether our home is at peace or at war, and whether power is wielded abusively, coercively or democratically. We tend to replicate these external leadership role models within the psyche, creating the extremes of harsh army boot camps, critical court-room judges, or constant exam rooms. At the other end of the spectrum we may replicate weak external leadership models with psychological ghost towns where nobody is in charge, internal communities where 'anything goes' and entitlement runs rampant. Both ends of this spectrum often lead to anxiety, and many of us have internal leadership that lies somewhere along this continuum.

The ruler within

Uncovering the way in which we rule our psyches can be a radical moment in therapy, largely because that rulership often runs counter to our sense of identity. Most people do not suspect that they are a ruthless army major or an ambivalent, absent president. In fact, it is usually a surprise for clients to even think about the type of leadership or political rulership that they practice internally. Uncovering wounds and understanding their nature and significance is not enough; we must also decide and put into practice the type of attitude that we wish to take towards that wounding, and thereby increase our internal compassion or increase our internal hostility to ourselves, and therefore to others.

Effective therapy both role models and enables that process of regime change. Our brains continue to have a degree of plasticity throughout our lives, and a therapist's way of being and relating can have a profound impact on the way in which clients relate to their own wounded landscape, and in turn to the prevailing way in which they relate to what matters most, and therefore what can hurt the most, for others. The potential domino effect of passing on compassionate resilience within relationships in this way can positively affect family life, friendships, work places and partnerships of all kinds. In this way, therapy is not just about the individual, it is about world work, in that it encourages fair, informed, compassionate and decisive leadership in the people who choose to engage honestly and courageously with themselves.

Forays into wounded territory have the potential to strengthen therapeutic alliance if the client feels allied by the therapist: important stories will be uncovered, shared and their significance honoured, with more constructive leadership attitudes to those stories being developed and practiced. Those moments often strengthen a client's sense of their own courage and ability to face other potential challenges in their life, as they realize how much they have already faced, and this in turn can increase self-worth and self-respect.

Addressing someone's front of house chosen identity, exploring contact styles and attachment preferences, engaging with the defences that keep them safe, and making forays into the wounded territory where important meaning making can occur, may be the sum total of a good piece of therapeutic work. For some client work, though, there is an additional layer of work that might unfold at this point, should they wish to engage with it, and that is the existential landscape.

After much hard work in therapy, a client may come into the consulting room and say they feel better equipped to deal with their presenting issues, that they have made the changes to their lives that they wanted to, and that it may be time to end. Other clients might come to a session one day, especially if they have been working in therapy for a while and after a period of heightened gains and say 'I have been feeling pretty good whilst I have been working with you, but suddenly I feel really flat. What is the point of all this working on myself? I am still here with all my flaws and my relationships are still difficult. No matter what I change, life is still hard.' At this point, there is either a need to reinforce or re-explore leadership attitudes towards their limitations as a human being, or you are on the cusp of the next layer of the psyche – the meaning making landscape that is existential terrain.

Existential Territory

For some people, existential territory arises after a period of heightened achievement, or a peak of creative expression. The wintery feeling that follows such output can leave us feeling empty and as if we have nothing else to give. For others, it is a developmental period during mid-life when parents are moving into their senior years and we start to notice that there is more life behind us than ahead of us, and we begin to ask 'what has it all been for?'

Occasionally an individual's life is scattered throughout with an awareness of existential questions, particularly if they have encountered tragedy during childhood, so that the icy blasts of mortality, the reality of isolation, and the fundamental truth of our precarious vulnerability as human beings has come to their door far earlier than their developmental arc might have prepared them for.

With the onset of constant digital streaming of news to our phones, tablets and televisions, so that we can view tragic events unfold in real time, personal tragedy is no longer the only way in which we are exposed to the horrors that are around us: we also have access to the world media and therefore to the chaos, torture, terrorism, war and abuse occurring across the globe. Many clients who present with existential anxiety confide that they are affected by this stream of information along with resulting symptoms of obsessive-compulsive behaviour, intrusive thoughts, anxiety disorders and panic attacks. It is harder to maintain a healthy denial towards the constant possibility of death for ourselves and those we love, when so much evidence exists to the contrary.

The existential landscape

If existential anxiety is a client's presenting issue, or they have experienced a recent loss or face a life-threatening diagnosis, then you may find as a therapist that you are plunged into an existential landscape from the get-go. In this case, you will still begin by meeting the metaphorical outer wall of the walled garden, the client's defences and some of their wounded territory. However, when the imperative to engage with the often desert-like landscape when existential issues are thickly present, then everything takes on a heightened weight and a sense of both significance and emptiness.

The paradox of feeling that matters of extreme importance are occurring, whilst at the same time nothing seems to matter, is part of the atmosphere of existential themes. Within the desert, we can search and search for something we sense is there, only to uncover more sand. This can create panic; a sense that surely there is something meaningful and thirst quenching to be found, an oasis somewhere that has nourishment, comfort and a sense of purpose growing in it. Yet the more we seek, the less we find.

In existential territory the rules of therapy seem to be stood on their head; everything that might have been therapeutically effective before, no longer seems to work. When a client has worked long and hard on their wounding and developed a compassionate way of relating to themselves and others, then the depths of the existential question 'what's the point' - in the face of what cannot be changed, despite all the work on changing things that matter - follows close behind. In therapy, discovering what we have the capacity to change in ourselves can feel radical, liberating and dynamic. In existential territory, we enter a period of dark wisdom weaving, through developing the humility that comes from knowing we are very small in the grand scheme of things.

Given the meteoric rise in the publication and consumption of psychological and spiritual self-help literature, and the number of people who are finding their own sense of entitlement to be and do that which they aspire to, existential terrain can be a shock. We wish to feel that we can create the reality that we want, and when we are faced with what we cannot affect or change, we may descend into depression.

The opportunity within limitation

This part of therapeutic work can feel like the graveyard of hope, but perhaps more importantly, it can be the graveyard of rescue fantasies from the difficulties of life, exploding our secret bargaining with a powerful divine force to be spared loss, illness and tragedy if only we are good enough, spiritual enough, therapized enough, and hard-working enough. This arena cuts us down to size, reminds us that we are limited by our physical bodies, by the political, economic, educational, religious, cultural norms that we are born into or elect to join when we choose a home, work, family and role. No matter where we choose to be and what we choose to do, the limitations of that framework will close in and remind us that our greatest freedom lies not in what we can change 'out there', but in the attitudes and internal freedom granted in the way that we relate to ourselves and the world.

The tasks in this landscape are to first and foremost tolerate it, because every cell of our being as therapists may urge us to 'do something' when a client feels crushed by reality, leaving them feeling flat, anxious and depressed when facing the unchanging nature of the world around them. It can feel counter-intuitive to 'be with' these states, with compassionate interest and a sense that there is nowhere to go except to be in the here and now. This is more easily achieved if we ourselves as practitioners have experienced periods of facing death, isolation and the true nature of what 'freedom' means. These bottom line truths can feel frighteningly bleak. Yet, if we stay with reality as we are presented with it, there can be a loosening of grandiosity, a puncturing of omnipotence, and with it an emerging awareness that there is a vaster, natural mystery, timing and season to things that operates independently of our wishes, demands and expectations.

This sense of mystery does not have to have a faith attached to it, nor do we need to spiritualize the universe in which we live if that is not our way. Just the fact that the seasons keep changing, that political systems grow and die, that the people we love grow, evolve and sometimes falter, is enough of a mystery in and of itself. Life is, in everything that is evidenced, a cycle of growth and death. And whether we are choosing to engage with a galactic meaning making or a terrestrial meaning making of our own design that brings a sense of purpose to the nuts and bolts of our everyday encounter with existence, choose we must, at some point.

Our capacity to be co-creative with the opportunities and the limitations of the contexts we live within is an important part of feeling alive, engaged and sane as human beings. Our ability to get reality checks, to work within the feedback that life gives us, to see how we fit with others, to compromise when we must, to be aware of the small things that matter, and to be compassionate towards the frailty of the human condition, all depend on our willingness to acknowledge and engage with existential themes. This gives us the fortitude, strength and will to continue to choose life, with all its flaws, and to relate to others from a place of connectedness and collaboration.

Because with all our differences and uniqueness as humans, we are all connected by the simple facts that we must strive to survive: that we will experience love and loss, that we must choose roles in the cultures in which we live that may bring us more or less satisfaction, that we may suffer physically, mentally, emotionally, and spiritually and potentially fail to be and achieve all that we wanted to, by the time we face death. Existential truth levels the playing field of what it is to be human, and although money and privilege can soften the blow for a while, the fact of our mortality, and the sharp relief that our lives are thrown into as a result, is something that nobody escapes.

Surrendering and connections

Due to the reality that existential themes can ultimately bring us to our knees in terms of acknowledging our humanity, it is from there that we often experience our connection to other people and to a vast mystery that turns despite our requests, input and bargaining. These moments are possible to cultivate if a client is willing and able to stay in therapy during periods of existential inquiry with a therapist who doesn't derail the process by beginning another foray into wounded territory, which may at that point be more about 'doing', to avoid 'being with' the emptiness of existential themes.

During periods of surrendering to existential themes in therapy, as we accept the smallness of our existence in the face of the vastness of 'it all', something transpersonal begins to emerge over the edge into the next layer of the metaphorical walled garden of the psyche. Paradoxically, the emergence of transpersonal experience in the existential desert seems to operate as a state of grace, when both client and therapist have released attachment to outcome, surrendering to what is, and yielding to realities too large to fully comprehend. At this point, a transpersonal, liminal atmosphere or state can enter the consulting room.

Transpersonal Territory

As with all the other levels that we have explored in this chapter, transpersonal territory is of course not confined to one area of our psyche's landscape, just as our relationality, defences, wounding and existential experiences are not confined to any one stage of therapy. The psyche is available in all its forms at any given time, hence the need to differentiate and focus on the type of material that is most useful to engage with as therapy progresses.

It is therefore a given that the transpersonal is present all the time. In Chapter Two I discussed field theory and the way in which that interfaces with transpersonal themes; indeed, whenever we speak about 'what is emerging', we are to a degree using transpersonal language and concepts. This is because, whether we are working from a conscious or unconscious position, there is an intelligence of some kind, or structure of some sort, from which process evolves.

The unconscious itself is a mystery that we barely understand; thus, books such as this one are simply stabbing in the dark when attempting to bring structure to the vast ocean of what we do not know. Consequently, the main thrust of this book is to offer ways of finding the edge of where we are at any given moment: the edge between what we are comfortable with (the known) and what we are uncomfortable with (the unknown). We may then learn to notice, inquire into, and relate to what comes over the edge from the unknown, despite our discomfort. Perhaps that is all therapy can ever offer: a frame in which we contract to facilitate the unknown and attempt to integrate it in a way that makes sense to our prevailing status quo.

Describing the transpersonal

Putting words to what we mean by the transpersonal is a tricky business, because no language effectively embodies and sufficiently encompasses it. And yet, conceptual, metaphorical language that attempts to describe an experience is our tool as talking therapists. So, within the limitations of that language, therapists must venture into the arena of describing altered states: atmospheres where synchronicity occurs; unusual events and experiences which make no sense to our rational minds; states of grace where changes and healing seem to enter our spaces without invitation or effort; feelings of peace, joy, contentment with ourselves; and being in exactly the right place, at the right time, and connected to something profound that we cannot explain, but nevertheless feels very real.

These kinds of descriptions are one of the reasons why transpersonal approaches have sometimes been scoffed at by other therapeutic modalities, and transpersonal psychotherapy has been accused of being fluffy, flaky, avoidant of the real meat of true depth work and failing to account for itself clinically with what it means by 'the transpersonal'. However, having taught therapists from multiple modalities for many years, I have witnessed a regular sharing of client work from practitioners who have described unusual states or atmospheres which have occurred spontaneously during their sessions, which they have noted privately but felt embarrassed to take to supervision due to their struggle to explain it in status quo clinical terms.

In truth, many people train as therapists after encountering a sense of being called to the work, to serve in some way, which they later describe in training or supervision contexts as having forgotten about or dismissed once their clinical training started, as it seemed childish or silly. In the effort to professionalize the therapeutic world it may be that we have also created a 'group edge' whereby we seek analytical concepts that give us a secure sense of our role and task, forgetting that it was the mysterious transpersonal quest for meaning and purpose that drew us to the work in the first place.

As therapists, if we wish to effectively facilitate the spontaneous moments where clients feel deeply connected to themselves and the world around them, we must risk sounding odd or admitting that we are in unfamiliar territory where something important is occurring that we do not understand, but can certainly welcome, be with, and encounter with humility. During these times, clients can move right into the centre of themselves, lit from within with a renewed sense of calm, peace, gratitude, compassion, power, inspiration and certainty. These are not the manic states of psychosis; they are often quiet states that bring a sense of certainty to the client, of 'rightness'.

Supporting ourselves and our clients to stay with these states of being – and finding words to describe what is occurring – helps to anchor the experience in the here and now of the relational space, giving us as therapists a sense of what is going on for the client. Learning to describe, rather than analyze, is the most important tool to develop when working with transpersonally charged moments in therapy. If the therapist can become the 'storyteller' who meta communicates (describes) what is occurring, rather than analyzing it, processes can unfold relationally without interruption. Clients can internalize that capacity and practice being the 'storyteller' in their own experience, building upon their ability to be compassionate leaders within their internal worlds, accompanying their own process without assessing and commentating on it.

Psychotic states

Because transpersonal moments can be confused with psychotic states, let's differentiate the two in simple terms. The most obvious thing to say here is to notice your countertransference as a therapist. In simple terms, if you are faced with a psychotic client, it is possible that the hair will be standing up on the back of your neck along with countertransference feelings of paranoia and anxiety. Conversely, if you are with a stable client who is experiencing a transpersonal state, you are likely to be feeling relaxed, connected, illuminated and calm.

If we go back to the edge work in Chapter 3, and we map a client who presents with psychotic tendencies or develops psychotic tendencies during a course of therapy, these clients will often have a fragmented and undefined 'me' sense of identity. They will struggle to cope with their therapist's input, feel easily invaded or offended, and may over-react to what their therapist says and does. These clients may obsessively analyze the world around them in a paranoid way, full of fantasies about what others think of them or wish to do them, and there is often an unwillingness or refusal to participate in reality-checking dialogues with their therapist. Finding mutual ground will be difficult with these clients as they become agitated by input that has come from anyone other than themselves, and feelings of walking on egg-shells is common for their therapists. These reactions are also found in personality-disordered clients who resist therapy from early on, even though they have willingly signed up for it and say they want to attend.

What is over these clients' edges are often split off, hostile, chaotic and vulnerable ways of being that the client feels swamped by, which are projected out into the world as ever-present hostile attacks. Grandiosity and omnipotent fantasies may persist, along with feelings of being lost in dissociated states due to an undeveloped sense of self and poor internal boundaries between conscious and unconscious material. This means that the initial work at hand is to ensure that they are properly assessed by a mental health team who can ascertain their capacity to function and possibly prescribe medication to target escalated, hyper-vigilant states.

Therapists then need to work in a grounded here and now way, focusing on what is going on in the room: staying with evidenced reality; working with the relational space in terms of what is occurring between therapist and client; and supporting the client to define themselves in an ordinary, down to earth way, rather than getting lost in merged fantasies of what may be going on for others. Facilitating an individuating, differentiating developmental process is the task.

Transpersonal states

A stable client who is entering a transpersonal state has a clearly defined sense of 'me' identity, with an ability to engage in mutual, reality checking dialogue with their therapist as well as showing an ability to be receptive to others input and thoughtful in their responses. There is usually a sense of the transpersonal state coming 'to them' and then leaving, as if a moment of illumination has occurred. Such clients are still able to go about the business of their lives, but report experiencing more contentment, acceptance of what is, less defensiveness, and more of a desire to listen to and support others without feeling curbed in their own self-expression.

Clients who have been willing to move through earlier stages of therapy where they are able to contact a range of emotions and both agree and disagree with their therapist – and survive both – are on more solid ground. These clients demonstrate an interest in exploring the story of their lives with dialogue and insight and they are relatively individuated in their ability to distinguish reality from their own internal commentary and fantasy. This client group is far less at risk of psychotic episodes. For these people, transpersonal states of 'knowingness', peace, and compassion, will be beneficial, enhancing and life affirming.

The task in this phase of the work is simplicity. Many transpersonal approaches claim to teach ways of contacting the transpersonal through visualization, bodywork and other focusing techniques. However, whilst these tools are extremely useful, they usually elicit material that belongs to other parts of the metaphorical walled garden and their greatest use is to help a client to build a bridge between their cognition and emotion through developing their imaginal capacity. Developing the imagination and incorporating the use of symbol, metaphor, myth and image is the fastest way to circumvent cognitive defences and does not require a client to feel something if they do not have access to a felt sense.

Truly transpersonal moments tend to occur spontaneously, without being sought after; as therapists we can cultivate the ground to encourage such moments, but we certainly cannot construct it through the mechanical use of techniques. The part that imaginal work can play in preparing the ground takes us on to the next chapter: archetypal perspectives on unfolding personal mythology.

---

[1] American Psychiatric Association, *Diagnostic and statistical manual of mental disorders (DSM-5®)* (Arlington, VA: American Psychiatric Publishing, 2013).

Chapter 5

Archetypal Perspectives on Unfolding Personal Mythology

In his book, 'Psychosynthesis: A Manual of Principles and Techniques', Roberto Assagioli describes the use of waking dreaming as a way of evoking both the personal and collective unconscious and engaging with collective archetypes which may be influencing our lives and experiences, thereby taking more mastery of them.[1] For Assagioli, there is a clearly defined need to have a full and thorough exploration of a client's personal unconscious before engaging with more collective unconscious, archetypal material. He did not propose using meditative techniques as a way of bypassing the significant landscapes that are outlined in the previous chapter. He did however see the benefits of meditative techniques to activate unconscious material once the strength of the client is deemed to be ready for it.

> There is value in the analysis of abnormality, but emphasis on the analytical is usually emphasis on our psychic past. During meditation, there is more dependence on the tendency toward health in the psyche. The orientation is synthetic rather than analytic.[2]

Roberto Assagioli (1888–1974) and Carl Gustav Jung (1875–1961) were both pioneers of transpersonal psychology; both men, within their own evolving therapeutic approaches of psychosynthesis and analytical psychology, utilized concepts of the collective unconscious and archetypes.

> The collective unconscious and archetypes are ancestral inheritances that have universal meaning and are in

themselves beyond the personal dimension (Jung, 2012). Archetypes have both transpersonal and personal expressions, and they provide a context for understanding the historical evolution of the mind and its spiritual-transpersonal experience... Assagioli agreed with Jung on there being a collective-archetypal unconscious beyond the personal unconscious, but he developed a systematic approach to the transpersonal domain with an emphasis on the experience of its distinctive "contents".[3]

In current psychosynthesis trainings, the role of archetypes tends to be omitted, perhaps because Assagioli himself downplayed archetypal themes for fear that the material might discredit psychosynthesis as a legitimate psychotherapeutic approach. In contrast, Jungian approaches are more interested in explicitly examining archetypal themes, possibly as a result of Jung being explicit about his experience of the archetypal world, and its significance. Psychosynthesis tends to focus instead on work with subpersonalities, a concept used to describe the multiplicity of different personalities within the psyche. In the consulting room, a subpersonality that may be dominating a client's current experience might be identified, explored, and worked with as a personality within its own right in the client's psyche, with its own way of being, moving, and behaving, and possessing its own belief systems. Psychosynthesis approaches encourage clients to create a dialogue between these different parts of themselves, with the hope of creating a greater degree of negotiation and cooperation between them, thus reducing internal conflicts and creating a greater sense of personal cohesion.

In Chapter 2 we explored the possibility that subpersonalities might be influenced by archetypes within the collective unconscious, especially as subpersonalities are often personal expressions of archetypal ways of being, as archetypes represent fundamental and universal patterns and motifs within human nature. If subpersonalities are to be charged with more of the essential motifs that lie at the heart of them, deeper than their surface presentation shows, then we must engage with archetypal concepts more directly and bring them to the foreground in the consulting and training room. Perhaps it is seen as too abstract or 'out there' to work with archetypal concepts concretely; however, when we start to engage with the myths, legends and stories spanning centuries and nationalities, we can begin to see patterns that elevate our personal subpersonalities from quarrelsome and often estranged personality traits into characters that have purpose, tasks and contributions to the psyche as a whole.

> Subpersonalities are like the exiled gods – caricatures, degraded specimens of the original, luminous archetypes... subpersonalities are clearly susceptible to transformation. Instead of degraded archetypes, they can be regarded as psychological contents striving to emulate an archetype, as a gross version of what is to appear later in a much more refined form.[4]

I have found through my work with clients and in training groups comprising a range of practitioners with differing therapeutic theoretical backgrounds that there is a strong and welcome response to working with archetypal themes. Students describe a sense that the work is lifted from a purely personal perspective, which can be quite arid, into an alive space with more connection and rapid understanding of the concepts being discussed. Archetypes such as the Trickster, the Sage, the Lover and the Hero (to name but a few) evoke immediate responses and comprehension in people.

Rather than having to use many clinical words to describe a process, archetypal descriptions excite people, as there is mutual understanding, as well as an emotional response to these descriptive states. Much can be described in a short space of time using archetypal concepts, as archetypal names seem to embody whole ways of being, stories unfolding, tasks to be faced, and ways of relating that many people are able to grasp more easily than complicated theory. Archetypal descriptions ignite memories of childhood stories, films, books, plays, songs and all forms of art that carry these essential patterns of being imprinted within them.

Archetypal envelopes of influence

Working with archetypal concepts addresses the collective unconscious as a field of influence in an individual's psychological landscape.

For the sake of differentiation, we can place archetypal influences into two categories:

- **Developmental archetypes**. These archetypes are denotated by developmental phases, such as the Maiden, Princess, Prince and Knight archetypes in young people during their 20's that need to develop into Queens and Kings as they struggle on the edge before leaping into building a dominion at work and in the home. Or the Sage, the Crone, the Wise Man and Wise Woman that seek to come foreground during the developmental stage of transitioning from middle age into the later stages of our lives.

  At each developmental stage, we experience the usual hesitation at the edge of transition from one way of being to another, simply because we have a tendency as human beings to stay with the familiar and resist the unknown. This may be the influence of the oldest part of our brain that orients around survival and is activated towards keeping us in known territory so that we do not put our lives in danger. This part of the brain continues to interpret new experiences as a threat to our survival and safety. Additionally, our edge figures have attachments to behaviour that is acceptable to our existing tribe and sense of identity ('me'), constantly convincing us that moving into an unknown developmental phase will bring dire consequences to the existing status quo. Developmental archetypes are more like the qualitative shift that we face during key transitional times, which are in part shared by us all. These developmental phases, and their accompanying shift in archetypal qualities, often ignite and evoke the core archetypes within our archetypal envelope.

- **Core archetypes in our archetypal envelope.** These are archetypes whose core themes circulate in a person's life from birth onwards. The cultures and families that we are born into bring powerful influences to bear in shaping us into who we will become, yet core archetypal influences can be shared across cultural and class divides, creating a type of subjective tribe that people may have more in common with than they might do with their own cultural tribe.

An example which illustrates core archetypes that are shared by people from different backgrounds are two clients who appear to have the archetypes of the Hero and the Warrior strongly influencing their life story and the fate or destiny within the challenges that they face:

- One client comes from a privileged, wealthy background but is born with a congenital condition that affects his coordination and mobility. He receives physiotherapy and occupational therapy to help him improve his coordination, but his ability to play sports continues to be hampered. Then, at the age of 7, he is sent to boarding school in line with his family's traditions, where he experiences a lot of bullying from other boys due to the school's strong emphasis on sporting achievements. This drives him to learn to stand up for himself, to use relational skills (rather than sporting activities) that make it possible to bond with other boys, and he develops his own true passion in science. In later life he goes on to groundbreaking territory in his chosen profession and founds a programme for scientifically gifted young people.

  This client has been born into privilege, but with a fate that means he must face being marginalized. As with all Heroes' journeys, there is a huge challenge to overcome, not of the Hero's making, and the Warrior in him must become activated so that he can stand his ground and forge his own path away from the status quo. The Warrior fights internal demons as well as external foes, and he finds the courage to be himself in the face of humiliation. As the Hero, he uses what he has learned on his own path in service to others in his adult life.

- The second client comes from a family who run their own family restaurant as first-generation immigrants; home life is very much overlapped with work life, especially as they live in a flat above the restaurant. There is strong pressure to work in the restaurant as she grows up, which she enjoys. However, she is offered a scholarship opportunity to study applied mathematics at the university of her choice, which is far away from home and, if she attended, she would be the first person in her family to get a degree. Her family do not want her to go and see her as essential to the future of the restaurant as she has a flair for cooking, handling customers and maintaining the accounts. Her parents have been open with her in assuming that she would take over the running of the restaurant, particularly as her mother has recently received a diagnosis of breast cancer.

  The client feels extremely conflicted but has a powerful urge to fulfil her passion at university and develop a career that she has planned for herself. For a while, this means that her relationship with her family breaks down and she is shunned as being 'selfish'. This is a painful time for her, as she goes it alone on her chosen path, until several years later when she has the courage to make an unplanned visit to her parents' home. Her mother's condition has worsened and her reunion with her parents is a difficult one, but she persists with building bridges and is able to have some rapprochement with her mother before she dies. This client's fate in life and the strength and courage needed for her to carve her own path away from the status quo of her family, risking being excommunicated by her tribe in order to fulfil her own sense of purpose, evidences the archetypes of the Hero and the Warrior.

People who share similar archetypal life stories often find that they have much in common, regardless of the differences in their cultural, economic and religious differences. The archetypal feel of our lives connects us deeply to both the challenges and tasks that face us, as well as 'that which cannot be changed', or the fate that we must also grapple with. The fate of someone's life, particularly as a child and adolescent, is an interesting red thread to notice, because it often highlights the archetypal influences at work, constructing the backdrop against which the individual will unfold their personal life story or life myth.

In this way, we might hypothesize that we all have an archetypal envelope of influence from our moment of birth, an almost tailor-made envelope containing the archetypal software that will begin downloading into our psyches through the catalyzing events of our lives. As therapists, when we listen to clients and map their processes, we can begin to see not just the ways of being and doing that are acceptable and unacceptable to them but also the archetypal qualities and characteristics that match those ways of being. If we regularly map clients as they share both their history and their everyday lives, we will begin to see the same archetypes coming up again and again. These archetypes are often in their archetypal envelope containing the key themes, challenges, tasks and contributions that they will grapple with throughout their lives.

Example of mapping archetypes

Let us look again at using edge work as an example of mapping a client, including adding the edge issues and potential archetypal qualities.

Example 1:

A client presents with anxiety and feelings of having lost touch with a sense of purpose in her life. She is a mother of two children aged 13 and 10 years old, has a senior job which carries a lot of responsibility, and is married to a man who also works long hours.

As she describes her life, I notice that she places great emphasis on blaming herself for how tired she feels and the squabbles in her marriage. She also experiences a lot of guilt regarding her working hours and tiredness at the end of her busy working days as a failure in terms of her role as a mother. This type of mother guilt is fairly normal, but the client uses her obvious intelligence to berate and punish herself for the challenges of family life, with no evident awareness that she is doing a good job at home and at work.

I notice the adjectives that she uses to describe herself, the force of the internally punishing voice that is evident when she describes having been irritated or snappy at home, and the fears that she expresses when describing being assertive at work, afraid that she will be judged as a tyrant for doing so. She hates herself for any fleeting feelings of wanting to escape her home and work life, if only for a few days to have a break, and despite the strong qualities that she judges in herself as qualities that others might dislike in her, I notice the passion and energy in her voice, the vibrancy of her dialogue with me and her responsiveness to observations that I offer to her. She enjoys contact in the therapy room that has traction, and comments that her anxiety has eased by the end of the sessions. In other words, she feels better not when she is soothed by me in a motherly way, but when I challenge her in a clear, articulate, direct manner.

Below is the diagram of my initial mapping of her process and the archetypes that might be associated with either side of her conscious and unconscious process, with the edge core beliefs, defence mechanism and edge figures that seem to be foreground in my initial sessions with her.

As with many people who suffer with anxiety, this client's internal hostility towards her own potency and power has created an edge that walls off her capacity to stand up for herself and to consequently respect herself for her own powerful capacity in the face of a demanding and overwhelming life. Cut adrift from her own spontaneity, which would allow her to bend with ever-changing circumstances, she has become brittle and easily broken. Her cynical realism is being held at bay with a determination to hold a positive and sunny disposition while what is being called for is more of a roar. Her descriptions of her family interactions indicate

Figure 9. The Edge map, client example 1.

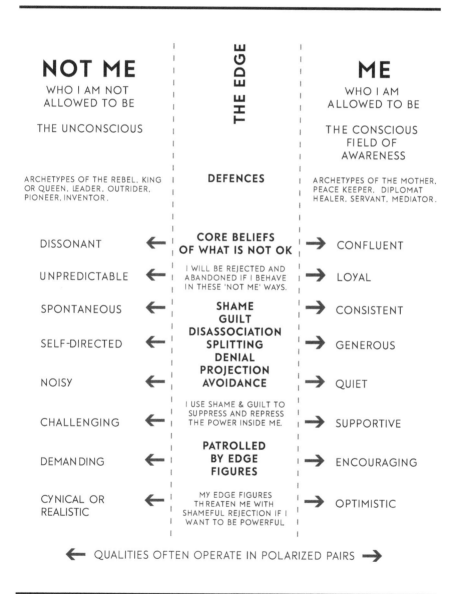

NOT ME
WHO I AM NOT
ALLOWED TO BE

THE UNCONSCIOUS

ARCHETYPES OF THE REBEL, KING
OR QUEEN, LEADER, OUTRIDER,
PIONEER, INVENTOR.

THE EDGE

ME
WHO I AM
ALLOWED TO BE

THE CONSCIOUS
FIELD OF
AWARENESS

ARCHETYPES OF THE MOTHER,
PEACE KEEPER, DIPLOMAT
HEALER, SERVANT, MEDIATOR.

DEFENCES

NOT ME		CORE BELIEFS / DEFENCES		ME
DISSONANT	←	**CORE BELIEFS OF WHAT IS NOT OK**	→	CONFLUENT
UNPREDICTABLE	←	I WILL BE REJECTED AND ABANDONED IF I BEHAVE IN THESE 'NOT ME' WAYS.	→	LOYAL
SPONTANEOUS	←	**SHAME GUILT**	→	CONSISTENT
SELF-DIRECTED	←	**DISASSOCIATION SPLITTING DENIAL**	→	GENEROUS
NOISY	←	**PROJECTION AVOIDANCE**	→	QUIET
CHALLENGING	←	I USE SHAME & GUILT TO SUPPRESS AND REPRESS THE POWER INSIDE ME.	→	SUPPORTIVE
DEMANDING	←	**PATROLLED BY EDGE FIGURES**	→	ENCOURAGING
CYNICAL OR REALISTIC	←	MY EDGE FIGURES THREATEN ME WITH SHAMEFUL REJECTION IF I WANT TO BE POWERFUL	→	OPTIMISTIC

← QUALITIES OFTEN OPERATE IN POLARIZED PAIRS →

THE EDGE
STACEY MILLICHAMP

that her children and partner would benefit from having clearer boundaries and for her to state her point of view more clearly. She identifies with being a slave at home who is taken for granted, whilst in reality her family look to her as the leader; a role that she shuns for fear of being viewed as too arrogant or forceful.

As seems to usually be the case with psychological material that is pushed into the unconscious, away from our conscious awareness, it becomes radioactive and begins to emit in covert ways. In this client's case, her power was emitting as silent resentment, sulking, panic and extremes of aggressive outbursts and withdrawal. Far from her anxiety being the cause of her inability to sleep, it was the tension of keeping her suppressed power under wraps that was keeping her awake at night.

Using this initial mapping, I role modelled being explicit, direct and assertive in my manner with her, as part of our task as therapists is be a conduit for 'not me' material to be safely aired in the room. The client responded positively to this by spontaneously identifying the ways in which she could become more explicit and direct in her relationships with others. She admitted her fears of being rejected if she was more powerful in her leadership roles at home and at work, and appreciated the opportunity to explore how direct communication, rather than covert requests, could be a more respectful and effective way of relating to others. We spent time challenging her edge figures' core belief that if she behaved in direct and challenging ways that she would be rejected by other people. Throughout the work she came to see that the people around her responded positively to knowing exactly where they stood with her rather than having to tiptoe around her, unsure of what she needed or wanted.

I have often found that when the archetype of the Mother descends on women, their previous ability to feel clearly outlined in who they are suffers a severe blow. Perhaps this is because the very act of motherhood, from pregnancy onwards, requires surrender to the needs of another. However, as children grow out of infancy and begin to flex their own muscles within the power dynamic at home, women feel challenged to regain the dominion that they once felt before they became mothers, in order to meet the emerging mini warrior within their child and to regain the chemistry that their pre-mother confidence had generated when they met their partner.

'Feeling into' the archetypes that lie over the edge, that are seeping through a client's covert signals, through encouraging the client to remember times in their life when they felt more of that quality, helps to ignite it again. Remember the field theory in Chapter 2 that reminds us that what we focus on within the field begins to wake up. In this case, the client spent time remembering her own rebellious freedom loving 20's, when she bravely headed towards the life she wanted, despite the setbacks that she experienced in her early home and school life, and we worked on what dominion meant for her as she explored becoming more of a queen within her own kingdom.

It is important to stress here that working with archetypes gives a therapist tremendous advantages in terms of dealing with edge figures in a client's process, because all archetypes have obviously positive qualities as well as shadow sides to them. Archetypes are fully rounded despite representing well-defined and distinct qualities of being and doing, and as 'characters' on our stage. These archetypes are magnetic and charismatic for clients, which makes it easier for them to open up to the unconscious 'not me' material that they so badly need to embrace to move forward with their lives.

Example 2:

A client in his early 20s presents with a tendency to burn bridges at work and at home. He has dropped out of education, become non-communicative with his family, and cannot hold down a job due to his 'bad attitude' and tendency to argue with his line managers.

The obvious way to work with a client such as this would be to trace back the way in which anger was expressed in his family of origin, and to address his anger-management issues. This would entail helping him to identify his trigger points and using cognitive behavioural approaches to equip him with the skills needed to de-escalate his temper from early on in his cycles of escalation. From an archetypal perspective, it is also useful to begin to map the way in which he sees himself and to hypothesize what the opposite end of those polarities might be, to get a sense of what is populating his unconscious 'not me' territory.

Having worked with a lot of clients who suffer with an inability to articulate and express what they are feeling and who therefore act out to show how they feel, I have found mapping to be particularly useful, as these clients do not naturally open up verbally in therapy. Making therapy useful for clients who are not 'talkers' means that we must bring structure into the space to help them make connections between their reactions and their ability to conceptualize and articulate. As therapists, hypothesizing for them and offering potential descriptions of what they might be feeling and experiencing gives them something to bounce off and offers new language to incorporate into their ability to think about and articulate their feelings.

This client is also an example of 'not me' unconscious material and associated potential archetypal influences, which represent ways of being and behaving that a client has struggled with and ultimately rejected during their childhood and adolescence. This client's parents, who were liberal in their politics and were teachers by profession, had striven to instil the values of justice, service and inquiry into him. He, however, felt that they were judgemental of him as a young man and naïve to the realities of the world that he inhabited with his friends from primary school onwards, where he was relentlessly bullied and consequently surmised that his ability to survive involved earning a reputation for being feared and not to be messed with. His parents' interventions at school had in his opinion, been feeble, and in fact had escalated the problem when the bullies at school jeered at him for being a 'mummy's boy'.

In rejecting his family values and relegating them to his unconscious 'not me' territory, he cut himself adrift from the archetypal figures that were seeking expression through his persistent challenge of authority figures at work, including on behalf of other employees whom he felt were badly treated or taken advantage of. As I listened to this client, I could hear his dilemma of both scorning his 'loony liberal' parents' attempts to help 'people who didn't deserve it,' whilst also bringing stories of how he had stood up for work colleagues – and risked his own employment as a result – as well as getting into violent altercations during his evenings out with friends through sticking up for the underdog.

His edge figures were ruthless in disallowing any vulnerability into his field of awareness and kept him enrolled in a metaphorical boot camp and permanently hypervigilant, waiting for the next attack from the world and working hard to act and relate in a way that emitted an ambivalent 'I don't care' attitude until he exploded into rage with people that he perceived to be bullying others. He was, of course, sticking up for others instead of sticking up for himself, but because he couldn't feel his own sense of victimization he preferred to live in a pumped-up state of being a rebel without a cause.

Every time he brought an example of his explosions, or the silent treatment that he had subjected someone to who had slighted him in some way, I inquired into what really mattered to him in those instances. I pointed out that his reactivity was related to his passionate caring about the way in which he thought people should be treated, and the way in which power was abused in the world. This made him pause for thought and, despite dismissing my observations on a regular basis, he eventually began to admit that he cared deeply about abuses of power and recognized this as a motivating force in his angry outbursts.

Below is my mapping of his process: this is a prime example of where wounding has occurred around transpersonal principles that matter deeply to a person. This client had buried what was precious to him deeply underground in his unconscious, so that he became a rebel without a cause. But as we began to excavate what he truly cared about, we came to recognize that the archetypes of the Justice Seeker, Mediator, and the Teacher were at play in the bones we unearthed in his wounded territory.

As he learned to articulate what mattered to him (rather than suppressing it), he became more skilful at supporting colleagues and friends who needed help to stand up for themselves. His self-respect grew as he experienced more mastery of his temper and

Figure 10. The Edge map, client example 2.

NOT ME	THE EDGE	ME
WHO I AM NOT ALLOWED TO BE		WHO I AM ALLOWED TO BE
THE UNCONSCIOUS		THE CONSCIOUS FIELD OF AWARENESS
ARCHETYPES OF THE JUSTICE SEEKER, THE TEACHER, THE MEDIATOR	DEFENCES	ARCHETYPES OF THE REBEL, THE LONER, THE OUTSIDER
MEASURED ←	**CORE BELIEFS OF WHAT IS NOT OK** →	ANGRY
RESPECTFUL ←	I WILL BE DAMAGED IF I SHOW THAT I CARE. I AM A FAILURE. →	DISRESPECTFUL
INSPIRED ←	**SHAME** →	AMBIVALENT
COMMITTED ←	**GUILT DISASSOCIATION SPLITTING** →	UNCOMMITTED
COLLABORATIVE ←	**DENIAL PROJECTION AVOIDANCE** →	REBELLIOUS
HOPEFUL ←	I SPLIT OFF MY PASSIONATE CARING BECAUSE I WILL BE HUMILIATED FOR APPEARING WEAK. →	HOPELESS
RELATIONAL ←	**PATROLLED BY EDGE** →	ISOLATED
VISIBLE ←	**FIGURES** →	INVISIBLE
	MY EDGE FIGURES THREATEN ME WITH VIOLENCE IF I LET OTHERS IN.	

← QUALITIES OFTEN OPERATE IN POLARIZED PAIRS →

THE EDGE
STACEY MILLICHAMP

therefore better outcomes when he stood his ground with authority figures. Eventually he took several courses on mediation and became a mentor for young people who needed the kind of psycho-education that he had accrued through his personal journey. He used his story as an inspiration for other young people who needed to know that there was hope for them in their lives.

Both clients in example 1 and 2 are experiencing developmental archetypes and core archetypes in their process, as both are moving into new stages of their lives where they are seeking to exert more of a sense of dominion. Due to them experiencing developmental shifts, their core archetypes are using the opportunity to push forward and support them to embrace their own uniqueness in the individual ways that they create healthy dominion in their own personal and professional territory.

As you can see, mapping is not as difficult as it might sound. It is simply a way of structuring what you are already doing as a therapist, creating a dynamic blueprint of the territory that you are excavating at any given time with a client. If you practice this way of mapping a client's process, it becomes easier and faster, and developing two types of attention becomes natural.

Our first attention is to the content that a client is bringing and the second attention is internally wondering what landscape we are in with our client – what characters are in that landscape; what tasks and relationships are happening there; and what type of police force patrols their landscape and keeps it under control.

As therapists, allowing an imaginal space to be operating at the same time as we are listening to our client's verbal content is extremely helpful, and mulling over imaginal content, archetypal characters and mythical landscapes is not something we need to close our eyes to engage with. Practitioners talk about noticing countertransference, but we can go much further and begin to put flesh and bones on the sensations, thoughts and feelings that we experience when we sit with clients. We can drop the need to be clever, complicating the space with analysis, and simply listen to what the client is telling us about their identity ('me'), the attitudes and behaviours that they don't like ('not me'), and then we can begin to map them.

Of course, some of the behaviours that both we and our clients don't like are important to consider in terms of being genuinely undesirable, such as violence, blaming, shaming and judging. However, if we relegate those behaviours to the unconscious they will operate outside of our awareness (because we cannot eradicate them entirely) and we miss the opportunity to elicit the archetypal transpersonal qualities that offer gifts within the distorted shadow element of themselves. For example, the healthy power hiding at the heart of violence; the intuitive descriptions of reality hiding at the heart of blaming; the healthy truth-telling that is at the core of shaming; and the clarity of discernment at the core of judging.

All archetypes have a distorted shadow, and a transpersonal purpose around which it constellates. Kings and Queens can be tyrants, Hermits can be hostile to the world, Justice Seekers can be judgmental and punitive, High Priests and Priestesses can be prostituted into selling their healing for the right prices, and Orphans can be restless loners. Therefore, if we dig into the gold buried underneath distorted archetypal behaviour and attitudes, we might unearth transpersonal principles that have the potential to unify and catalyze the meaning that is underlying and organizing the patterns of our lives.

The fate contained within our archetypal envelope

As we work on our edges and interact with the material that is emerging from our unconscious territory, we enlarge our conscious field of awareness. Edge work is not an either-or process that makes what is conscious or unconscious either wrong or right; it is an enlarging of the territory that we are aware of, leading to increased ownership of the many different 'ways of being' that constellate within us. This means that as we work on our edges and incorporate more of what is edgy for us, our edges move to other conflicts within our unconscious.

It is therefore extremely important to remember that once a major edge has been worked with for a while, that after a period of 'plateau' and stability, new edges start to form. Our personal journey of expanding into the personal and collective unconscious is one that is life-long, and the skills we learn in therapy to work with our edges allow us to continue to work in a more collaborative way with ever-moving edge material throughout our lives.

The archetypal material on both sides of any given edge usually contain inherited ways of being, with acceptable archetypal material on the 'me' conscious side of the edge and archetypes that we find more challenging on the 'not me' unconscious side. These 'not me' archetypes, which may both frighten and excite us, are often signalled in the 'fateful' elements of our lives from our birth onwards. These are the archetypes that we could describe as being within our 'archetypal envelope' and they tend to be ways of being, thinking, and behaving that continue to follow us like dark allies, challenging us to step into our potential through the span of our lives.

The archetypes that are core to us often evidence early on through the type of circumstances surrounding our mother's pregnancy; the type of birth that we experienced; the tribal position we were allocated amongst siblings and family; childhood illnesses or the illnesses (or deaths) of those close to us during childhood; congenital conditions that changed the way we related to life and others; gifts and talents that either separated us from our peer group or which evidenced initially as an impairment or aversion in some way; recurring dreams through childhood; and childhood circumstances that brought particularly intense experiences in a repetitive way.

Examples of the fate contained within our archetypal envelope (limited to four examples, amongst an unlimited number of variations):

- Archetypes such as the Sage, the Visionary, the High Priest/Priestess and the Healer can evidence in the lives of children who suffer childhood diseases or tragedies that separate them from their peer group and generate a more introverted way of being during a developmental period that would naturally be more extroverted and socially oriented.

- Archetypes such as the Artist, the Muse, the Scientist, the Teacher, Pioneer and the Magician can evidence through early explorative, creative talents that generate ways of encountering and experiencing the world. These talents may be kick started through unusual circumstances that differentiate the child from their peer group, forcing them to develop a strong sense of individuality, to provide the courage necessary to pioneer new ways of seeing and doing things.

- Archetypes such as the Mother and Father, the Healer, the Judge, the Prostitute (which contains the seeds of the High Priestess), the Orphan (which contains the seeds of the Mother and Father) and the Judge (which contains the seeds of the Fair Mediator) can evidence through early neglect, illness within parental figures early on in life, and other childhood circumstances where the child is forced to take on caretaking for themselves, other siblings and parents.

- Archetypes such as the Warrior, the King and Queen, the Leader, the Justice Seeker and the Knight can evidence through early challenges in relation to their birth, their family environment, and sometimes the culture that they grow up in, which force the child to learn to fight back against danger of some kind. This danger can show up through illness, accidents, major loss, educational challenges, bullying, abuse, war or a family disintegration of some kind.

Archetypes, whether they are more female or masculine in their orientation, operate in girls/women and boys/men alike. Whatever archetypes we are fated to encounter within our archetypal envelope seem to seek us out throughout our childhood and adult lives. As therapists, we can begin to map those red threads through the challenges that repetitively constellate for clients. A therapist can then begin to share their hypothesis with the client and to support them to work with those archetypes –

to cooperate with them, to see the gifts in them and, to a degree, to surrender to their on-going presence and the teaching that they bring.

Working with archetypes in a conscious way with clients

- Utilize cognitive behavioural approaches that offer a grounded inquiry into how a specific archetypal quality might be incorporated into the client's way of being, doing, and relating.

- Work with night-time dreams that a client brings. Use waking dreaming (visualizations) that invites a client to engage with an archetype that has been identified in the work. Lead them to interact with this archetypal quality as an imaginal figure, dialoguing with, relating to, and even identifying with the figure to feel how it is to be/move/ speak/behave as that figure.

- The therapist can embody the qualities of an archetype that is in a client's 'not me' territory, through using their tone of voice and their way of being and relating, such as becoming more direct and challenging with Warrior energy, sharing more intuitive senses, thoughts and feelings with High Priest/Priestess energy, and becoming more maternal or paternal with Mother and Father energy. These are just basic examples, as there are numerous archetypes that are seeking contact within a client's process and it is up to therapists to explore their own edges to ensure that they are able to include clients' archetypal material that they might themselves feel challenged by.

- When working with couples, a therapist can ask each person what qualities attracted them to each other and enlarge those qualities into archetypes that represent those qualities. Oftentimes someone is attracted to their own 'not me' material which is manifested in another person's way of being. This is particularly the case with the core archetypes in our archetypal envelopes, which we therefore have a fate to develop in ourselves. For example, if I have banished power to my 'not me' unconscious, as disallowed, I may be attracted to powerful people who are magnetic to me in some way.

In this example, I may have an immediate attraction to a powerful person that I am mesmerized by, until further into the relationship when I begin to get angry and judgemental towards the very archetypal quality that attracted me to them in the first place. Helping each half of a couple to acknowledge their initial attraction to key qualities in each other and encouraging them to go over their own edges to develop and express those qualities within themselves, rather than 'making wrong' those qualities in the other person in the same way that they have within themselves, can be an extremely effective way of working in couple therapy.

Couples may also have archetypes that represent the relationship itself with key tasks and challenges. Asking a couple what qualities seem to emerge again and again in their way of being together physically, emotionally, cognitively and in terms of the roles that the couple play in the world, helps to create a sense of mutual purpose and learning that can deepen bonding and a sense of 'what we are supposed to be encouraging each other with, rather than blaming each other for.'

- This way of working with archetypes in couple dynamics is also relevant as a perspective for working with groups. As a trainer it can be useful to employ an imaginal sense of the landscape that the group is in, asking what the key tasks are, where the key challenges lie, and where the group edges are. I have often found it to be the case that a group has shared edges around particular themes that consistently constellate, and that there is potential for the group to therefore support each other to cross those edges and develop more of the group's unconscious archetypal material that is emerging into the foreground for them. Trainers can simply retrieve that data imaginally, simply for their own information, and use it as a map for ways of shaping the teaching material to suit the dynamics of the group. Alternatively, if there is a group dynamic developing that needs attention, the trainer can share their imaginal material with the group, and encourage the group to find their own images that represent the group's process and what may be emerging over the group's edge.

This is an additional way of working for therapists which deepens the exploration of wounding to include a perspective that sees the archetypal encounter that is occurring at the heart of the fateful material that litters a client's wounded landscape. Far from minimizing or brushing over wounds, such a perspective often brings more gravitas and awe to the fate of a client's life, and can answer the question often asked, 'why is this happening to me?'

As clients pick up their core archetypal material and begin to own it in themselves, recurring problems often ease and they experience a greater sense of peace that 'this is who I am' and 'this fate now holds meaning for me, in terms of making me who I am'. Blame is therefore often retracted towards family, friends, or their circumstances, as a client feels more in contact with the journey that their fate has taken them on and the way in which their fate has made them the unique person that they are; they are more able to utilize what has been learned as a contribution to the world, rather than something to feel ashamed of, or secretive about.

There will be many therapists who will disagree with this perspective and accuse the approach as being a rationalization of pain and a way of avoiding the grief and loss inherent within it. To those therapists, I would return them to the chapter on the walled garden where it was highlighted that clients may only wish to explore the outer layers of their survival defences and wounded territory; in those instances an archetypal perspective is not a necessary way of working with clients, nor is it intended as an avoidant way of working with pain. Clients do need to face the truth of what has been painful for them and to excavate the bones within their wounded territory. However, to bring a sense of pattern and purpose to the presence and nature of those bones and the stories that they tell, an archetypal approach has the potential to offer clients a sense of individuation and wholeness towards their past, present and future, through connecting with an evolutionary sense of 'who am I and what my life is about'.

Ruthless edge figures

When we listen to a client, edge core beliefs and edge-figure attacks, bullying and hostility towards the client's unconscious territory are easy to hear when the internal commentary of the way they speak to themselves becomes evident in the consulting room; worst case scenarios, catastrophizing, intimidation, shame and guilt attacks and ominous atmospheres are all part of the edge figure's weaponry. Therapists are wise to remember that, as with the defensive territory in the walled garden, we must understand and ally with the way in which edge figures are seeking to keep the client safe, so that we have the leverage necessary to negotiate with them. Debates have their place in the consulting room, even edgy conflicts at times if it is in the service of taking on edge figures that need firm and fearless engagement from therapists.

Some clients do not just have bullying commentators as edge figures, they have terrorist-like, murderous figures inside who torture them if they even begin to have forbidden thoughts, feelings and behaviour from 'not me' unconscious territory. Psychopathology wisdom might view these edge figures as intrusive thoughts, sadistic-masochistic impulses, and obsessive-compulsive rituals or borderline tendencies. The defences that clients construct to blot out these ruthless edge figures can lead to serious addiction, self-harming, eating disorders and suicidal ideation; the fragmentation that accompanies a severely punishing regime might also evidence as mood disorders or personality disorders.

These edge figures may be constellated when a client has experienced early life caretakers and authority figures as being absent through illness, addiction, death, work, neglect or other extenuating circumstances or conversely when a client has experienced caretaking and authority figures as abusive, coercive, manipulative or violent through emotional, mental, physical or sexual abuse. If there has additionally been peer group abuse and rejection with accompanying wider world chaos then we have a client who has had to hastily construct internal authority figures who are bigger and more bad assed than the world that they've had to face, and that is when the punitive, hostage-taking edge figure grabs hold of the psyche.

This makes sense, doesn't it? If you have no one to stand up for you in a dangerous world, you are forced to construct an internal protector who is big, brave and strong. The fact that this constructed caretaker takes on extremely ruthless characteristics in the absence of any appropriate role modelling with a moderating principle, is understandable. At the time of construction, this ruthless edge figure might make the difference between psychological coherence and dangerous fragmentation of the psyche. But once it has served its purpose this figure might be ruling the psyche with an iron fist that is no longer relevant to the client's circumstances. If ruthless edge figures are creating a psychotic state for the client, the therapist must contact the consultant psychiatrist that is overseeing their care after collaboration with the client, or work with the client to contact their GP (or primary care doctor) with a referral letter suggesting that they be formally assessed. It is important under these circumstances that therapists take a multi-disciplinary, joined-up approach to a client's care.

Safeguarding the client is therefore the priority. For clients who are extremely fragmented, therapy must be reality-based, cognitively assessing what is actually occurring in the client's life and helping them to differentiate between actual events and their internal fantasy narrative. For these clients, looking at 'parts of themselves', including archetypal themes, is contra-indicated, with the emphasis instead being on building a stronger and more defined sense of self, enabling self-care, and activating positive self-regard.

If a client with ruthless edge figures is stable, a therapist can work with the client to begin to take back more control.

Ways of working with ruthless edge figures, with clients who are stable:

- Provide reality checks for the client that contravenes the edge figures' control, offering an attachment between therapist and client that offsets the edge figures' dominance in the client's psyche.

- Teach the client to get real time, evidence-based reality checks for themselves so that they are less reliant on their edge figures' version of reality.

- Work with the client on developing internal leadership that reflects a compassionate, inspirational way of leading, rather than the punitive dictatorship that their edge figures have constructed. Provide psycho-education through assessing different leadership regimes and the way in which repressive regimes function as opposed to democratic regimes (despite their flaws). Help clients to think about leaders in the world that have inspired them and work on developing their healthy leadership styles internally and externally.

- Role model wise, strong leadership that is collaborative, honest and effective.

- Encourage the client to become aware of their internal edge figure commentator and the way that the commentator talks to them/threatens them. Practise replacing or over-writing this commentary with a realistic, objective, evidence-based commentary. This catalyzes the client to move away from listening to the edge figure commentary as 'the voice of authority' towards a relationship with the edge figure that is more challenging and objective (disidentified).

- Understand the purpose of the edge figure's approach towards the client, through discussing what necessitated the construction of a powerful dictator internally to 'look after' the client when the external world was too dangerous to cope with. It is not necessary to 'go into' those experiences or events, as simply identifying them is sufficient to activate understanding and the building of internal psychological support. Along with support must also come empathy for the client's current experience of finding the edge figure to be too ruthless and unnecessarily punitive, as well as truth telling that there are more effective ways for the client to look after themselves.

Populating psychological landscapes with archetypes and expanding them into mythological journeys

Putting together some of the approaches that we have explored in the previous chapters, we can use the archetypes that we have mapped with clients and choose to put them into a psychological landscape that describes the way in which the client is experiencing themselves at any given time. This is a way of interrogating the field that is constellating, assessing which part of the walled garden we are in, conceptualizing the relational dynamics at play, and opening to the archetypal space.

As therapists, we can utilize our own imaginal attention whilst listening to a client, which means developing our capacity for dual attention during sessions; the first attention notices the client's content while the second attention notices process information, utilizes our imaginal senses, and develops an internal narrative.

Using our second attention we can internally ask 'what landscape do I see this client in? What is occurring in this landscape? What of importance is happening here?' Any stage of an internal inquiry for the therapist can provide imaginal, process-oriented content that might bring illumination to the content that the client is presenting. It is not necessary to share this information with the client if they are not open at that time to imaginal work;

the therapist can simply utilize the metaphorical themes to punctuate the descriptive language employed in their interventions with the client as they respond to the material being presented in the room.

However, I have found that even cynical clients respond positively to a natural introduction of 'the mythical drama' potentially present within their material, especially if the therapist lets them know that this is their symbolic sense of the client's key themes. As with anything, a therapist can metaphorically throw the client a ball and if they pick it up and run with it that's great; if not, the therapist still benefits from not being held hostage in their own inner world by the content in the room, because they are internally able to move around with it and relate to what is presented in a variety of different ways.

I have heard many therapists describe burn out, not from stress but from the experience of being pinned to the same spot for hours at a time during client work, if they do not allow their internal imaginal world the freedom of a responsive, reflective experience of the concrete content being presented. Imaginal work offers a more enhanced way of working with countertransference than is often practiced in an analytical way, which can be somewhat reductive if emotional responses to the client are solely used as clues to unexpressed primitive material or unresolved relational issues from the past.

For example, a client that I had worked with for a long time had become astute and psychologically minded throughout her therapy, and as she progressed towards ending therapy she suddenly became argumentative with me during several sessions. I initially wondered whether the thought of leaving was re-stimulating the early autobiographical material with her family that we had worked with over a long period of time, but I noticed gladiatorial images coming to mind as we entered a conflict. When I shared this with her she smiled with recognition and said that she wanted to fight with me, not because she was afraid of leaving therapy but to show me that she could now stand up for herself and wanted to practice sparring in a healthy and respectful way. There was additionally a developmental archetype around of the

Prodigal Son/Daughter who was leaving home to go out into the world on a quest. This client was also actively in her core archetypes of the Gladiator and the Truth Teller, which had led her to be the black sheep of the family when she was young but which she was now learning to embrace from a place of capacity and awareness inside of herself.

We can facilitate the client to have an imaginal journey by asking them specific questions that activate their own inner inquiry. The client can have their eyes open or closed and it is helpful to ask the client to describe what is happening, as it occurs. I strongly suggest that as the therapist you still engage with your own imaginal responses to these questions while you are also offering them to the client, so that you might add your images to the client's during the guided imagery or compare them during the de-brief; this brings a relational element to intra-psychic work that helps the therapeutic relationship to navigate around the unconscious landscape that you are exploring. The following questions are offered as one example of how to unfold mythical landscape, but I would invite you as practitioners to develop your own and to allow the client's inquiry to expand on the basis of the images that they are recounting to you.

- 'I'm going to invite you to find yourself in a landscape. Look around and describe to me what this landscape looks like. Is it a city scene, a desert, a mountain range, the ocean, a garden, a house, or other landscape? Notice the colours, structures, smells, sounds and atmosphere of this place and begin to explore it'.

- 'What is occurring in this landscape? What characters do you see here, what tasks are being worked on, what relationships are occurring, what is being exchanged?'

- 'Where is the obstacle, conflict, or dilemma in this landscape? Who is engaged with, or trapped in, this part of the landscape?'

- 'Who in this landscape holds the key to unlocking the obstacle, conflict, or dilemma?'

- Work with night-time dreams with the client, whether current dreams or recurring childhood dreams.

- Explore fairy tales, fables, legends, films, books and other narratives that most affected them as children, or which most affect them now. Which character did they identify with? What were that character's mythological tasks and challenges, and what allies and qualities did they need to engage with the obstacles that faced them?

Actively supporting the client to practice using their imaginal capacity helps them to utilize the Storyteller archetype, providing an observational capacity that is not taking sides within their own landscape, instead narrating what is unfolding there. This helps to moderate the analytical assassinations of edge figures, by developing a descriptive capacity rather than therapy providing more analytical weapons in the edge figure's arsenal. I have seen many clients who have been in long-term therapy using the analytical concepts that they have learned there to cut themselves into analyzed pieces, and whilst it is helpful for clients to learn to think about and reflect on themselves, analytical scalpels when utilized by our edge psychopathology are not helpful.

You may often find that if you use this imaginal inquiry, either inside of yourself as the therapist or collaboratively with the client, that you find repeating stories unfolding. These stories often reflect the activities of the client's core archetypal envelope. Such reflections can provide a sense of purpose and illumination towards obstacles that clients are facing in their inner lives, their work and their relationships. Myths, as well as symbols, seem to have the capacity to represent the multi-level themes going on for clients. Symbolizing the nature of the journey in specific ways helps us as therapists to perceive the way in which apparently unrelated content is in fact connected. It also supports us at moments when we can feel very stuck, unable to understand why a client is circulating around and around an issue, with no apparent way to break more deeply into what is perplexing them. This way of working also reminds us as practitioners that the power of a client's personal mythology is far larger and more profound than we will ever fully understand.

Clients will often report that being related to in this way brings a special sense of feeling deeply 'known' and understood by their therapist, as clinical concepts are replaced with words and images that they can relate to, freeing them to experience themselves as part of something meaningful and significant.

Making your own list of archetypes and stories/fairy tales/folk tales/legends/fables

I have had many students and practitioners come to me after trainings to say that they do not know many fairy tales or fables, and that they are afraid that this will limit their capacity to work with archetypes and mythology. It is important to point out that it is not necessary to be an expert in ancient mythology or to have read lots of books on archetypes in order to work with this material.

We all have stories and narratives that we picked up as children from storybooks, films, or television series, many of which are peopled with versions of archetypes that are relevant to the world that we live in today. Even well-known people in the media can represent archetypes if we start asking which qualities and ways of being those people have that we look up to, admire or dislike. If you wish to explore further there is a bibliography at the end of this book that suggests some reading material.

If this material feels alien or too 'out there' for your practice, I encourage you to begin to give it a try and listen to the feedback that your clients give you. Their opinion is what matters most, and if they find this addition to your way of working a useful experience, be courageous and jump in more fully!

Working in this archetypal way with people may sometimes generate conflict as archetypal polarities can be constellated in the consulting room, in a heightened way. Real time relationship that explores these dynamics is vital if we are to be catalytic as therapists, rather than insisting that the client both catalyzes and relates to their own conflicts, without our presence in the battle. This takes us on to the next chapter: developing leadership within the psyche.

[1] Roberto Assagioli, *Psychosynthesis: A Manual of Principles and Techniques* (London: Thorsons, 1993), pp. 309 – 311.

[2] Assagioli, *Psychosynthesis*, p. 314.

[3] Massimo Rosselli and Duccio Vanni, "Roberto Assagioli and Carl Gustav Jung", *The Journal of Transpersonal Psychology* 46 (2014), p. 8.

[4] Piero Ferrucci, *What We May Be: The Vision and Techniques of Psychosynthesis* (London: Mandala, 1990), p. 55.

Chapter 6

Developing leadership within the psyche

Challenges within the therapeutic relationship

Therapeutic exploration usually has a primary objective of facilitating a separation individuation process for clients to mature into their capacity to more skilfully manage their internal worlds, external lives and relationships from a more self-aware perspective. The very nature of separation and individuation usually means differentiating 'you from me' and that entails facing the internal and external conflicts that arise as a result.

The context of a client's world may not support such emergence of individuality, rather requiring submission to a tribal status quo, and therapy might cause tremors in the existing structures of a client's life. Therefore, the therapy room must be the practice space where conflict can erupt, allowing truth telling that may be bruising to the therapist as well as the client, so that a middle ground position can eventually be found which is more effective and usable in the client's life.

I have many times heard students in training groups, or supervisees during consultations, articulate that 'I can't possibly say that' when it's been suggested that they find ways to directly communicate what they are thinking and feeling to a client. Practitioners are understandably afraid of causing offence or shaming clients in some way, and for that reason it is important to take things slowly, at a pace that allows careful attendance to signals of challenge in the room. Developing this capacity takes practice for the therapist, and that means we must start where we are able to and 'learn on the job'.

Having the courage to face our fears and practice in the moment with clients is worthwhile, because challenge offered in an insightful, relational way elevates therapy from useful to dynamically creative and catalytic. This is a viable alternative to playing it safe and avoiding potential conflict; putting the therapist on the same edge as their clients, who have come to therapy with a desire to create more intimacy and authenticity in their lives. More interestingly, we have the potential to offer people an alive, relational space in which to practice facing their fears.

Anger is acknowledged as being important by the therapeutic community, but is not often taught as being potentially catalytic; rather, it may be viewed as evidence of repressed material that needs to be expressed, or purely considered to be symptomatic of relational malfunctions from early life. Whilst those elements may be present, we could also view anger and passion as an everyday reality – with the need to fight for territory, for liberty, or for a cause that matters on behalf of ourselves and others – evidencing legitimate core values and ways of expressing in the world.

In my experience as a trainer and supervisor, I have found that many people who are drawn to the psychological, counselling and psychotherapy world are themselves afraid of conflict, and therefore avoidant of it. The Wounded Healer and Mediator archetypes are often actively engaged for therapists, rooted in wounding which may have involved an early life that required the development of intuitive satellite dishes, constantly on the look-out for conflictual signals in the field around themselves and others. Paradoxically, therapists are therefore best placed to mediate and soothe as a habitual reflex to any signs of provocation, rather than taking the more dynamic option of using their heightened ability to pick up conflictual signals and track conflict to its source. Turning this gift into a useable facility to head into provocation, rather than away from it, can be extremely redemptive for therapists.

Modelling conflict

Facilitating clients to become more 'psychologically intelligent' is not a sufficiently satisfactory therapeutic outcome. Psychotherapy needs to walk its talk and become better at modelling clean conflict, through a brave capacity to explore the truth within the relationship and to 'join in' with heightened moments in the consulting room. This allows clients to practice contactful ways of engaging with sticky moments in their relationships, rather than hypothesising about it.

Therapists need to be able to both feel the intensity that may be building for clients, whilst also having the ability to narrate it. The beauty of developing a first and second attention as clinicians is that it gives us the capacity to experience states that are present, whilst also describing them. This means that the practitioner is experientially present whilst also becoming the Storyteller of what might be emerging in the space between themselves and their clients. The same is also true of work with couples and groups, where conflicts often constellate and escalate more rapidly, requiring the therapist to pick up those escalating signals early on, whilst maintaining an ability to describe what is happening in the relational space between the people present.

Describing vs analyzing

Describing the space between people removes blame towards the origin of a conflict, and instead focuses on the brewing dynamic between people through meta communication of what is occurring. This means that no one person is burdened with being viewed as the cause or originator of that process. If therapy seeks to analyze the cause of a conflict and reduce it to one person's psychopathology, the 'field' that has constellated is split, creating a black-and-white, good-and-bad dynamic that inevitably leads to defensiveness and increased hostility. A field perspective that notices which roles are generated within a therapeutic relationship, couple relationship or group, is capable of naming what is arising, rather than seeking to find 'the cause of the problem' in a reductionist way.

A unit of work with an individual, couple or group might feel as if it has become a circular, repetitive process, at which point an edge needs to be identified and crossed in order to move things on. The most circular processes are often an avoidance of conflict and crossing that edge might involve the therapist noticing the provocation in the room and making it explicit or becoming provocative themselves.

A clumsy intervention that attempts to notice a tense atmosphere is better than no intervention at all, or an avoidant intervention that seeks to smooth things over. Pretending to ignore the aggression, sarcasm or patronizing behaviour that might be occurring in the therapeutic space is dangerous. Rather than creating safe ground, such avoidance will ultimately escalate the situation, because signals of 'heat' demand to be met; avoiding them or pretending that they don't exist will only exacerbate the situation.

An escalating conflict therefore requires that we 'hit the ground running' as therapists; feeling the anxiety and irritation internally, noticing the inflammation in the room, and moving to describe it and bring attention to it, even though we don't know why it is there. By taking this risk, each person in the dynamic notices that something important, but unknown, is occurring.

If the therapist additionally welcomes challenge and supports each side of the emerging conflict to speak and be heard, without a rush to premature resolution, then a conflictual encounter has the chance of becoming a moment of intimate contact. When differentiation is respected, unfolded, and encouraged, then it is often the case that mutual ground starts to emerge from the commonality of people caring deeply about their positions.

Caring deeply about something is an act of vulnerability. Having the courage to evidence passionate care is something that connects and touches people with a sense of what is meaningful, once the ammunition of blame is put away and an honest revealing of 'what matters to me' is shared. If conflict is not met with strong contact that mirrors its intensity, and a capacity to describe what appears to be occurring in the moment, then it will escalate or go underground, only to erupt at a later date. An unacknowledged conflict gives the message that it is not ok to tell the truth if it is unpalatable to others and leaves at least one side of the conflict resentful and withdrawn.

Conflict carries the potential to level the playing field, if people are willing to mutually seek for the truth in a situation, without being overly confined by polite role definition. Clients may unconsciously provoke conflict with their therapist in the hope of seeing what lies behind the therapist's professional façade, to unearth what they really think about the client. Couples bring conflict to therapy because they hope it is safe enough to tell the truth to their partner in a space that is strong enough to handle what might emerge as a result. Groups stimulate conflict because people long for, but have rarely experienced, well-handled, open, honest interaction in their family or peer groups. As a species that is so compulsively driven towards war, is it any wonder that conflict stirs in the therapeutic space in the hope that this time an honest interaction – one that does not involve being crushed by a more powerful other – might be possible?

Contact styles

We all have different contact styles, in other words, our preferred way of establishing and maintaining contact with others. If we refer to the outer level of the walled garden in Chapter Four, we remember that our contact style also relates to our 'front of house' face to the world. In the consulting or training room, when we first meet a client or teach a group, we can notice the way in which people set up the space with us because it describes a lot about their contact style and the types of contact boundaries that they may feel comfortable and uncomfortable with. In turn this gives us hints about their current edges, as they present their sense of personal identity – 'this is who I am' – in the signals that they give off with their body language, tone of voice, way of engaging us, and the material that they choose to offer first.

Dissonant and consonant

I am going to use a musical metaphor and suggest that our contact styles generally fall within a spectrum that extends between dissonant ways of relating and consonant ways of relating. Dissonance is a term that is used musically to describe a lack of harmony between musical notes, creating discordance. In terms of human behaviour, dissonance can be described as a lack of agreement or harmony between people – creating disagreement, difference, dissimilarity and contradiction. People who prefer this contact style are often differentiated in their way of relating, and will subtly or explicitly create distinct and different ground between themselves and others. Consonance is a term that is used musically to describe a combination of notes which are harmonious and similar. In terms of human behaviour, consonance can be described as accordance, unison and agreement. People who prefer this contact style are often confluent in their way of relating and are keen to create mutual ground between themselves and others.

The spectrum between dissonant and consonant ways of making contact is vast, and we move back and forth along that scale depending on the type of relationship that we are within. However, the type of contact that we generate when in a new, unpredictable situation tells us much about our default contact style. For dissonant types, differentiated ground that points to the differences between themselves and others feels the safest place to be and the consonant behaviour of others might be perceived as suffocating, patronizing or coercive. For consonant types, confluent ground that points to the similarities between themselves and others feels the safest place to be and the dissonant behaviour of others might be perceived as uncooperative, dominating and intimidating.

Our preferred contact style is influenced by the familial and peer group contact styles that we have experienced, with resulting attachment structures and conflicts between the need to belong versus the need for freedom. There are times within therapy to look closely at the way in which a client establishes contact, and the repercussions of that in their relational lives; but more importantly, knowing which contact style we fall into gives us the opportunity to understand and mediate our extremes in a way that can respect and meet others contact style if they differ from our own.

Couples and groups

Many painful misunderstandings arise between couples and groups due to the battle lines drawn between dissonant and consonant types. Many of us are unconscious of our own way of relating, which can lead to protracted and intractable circular processes where we attempt to persuade others that our way of creating contact is the 'right way'.

This is often an unconscious subtext to a lot of the arguments that couples have; not realizing that even though the subject matter might be about money, child rearing and who takes out the trash, the heart of the argument is constellated by attempts to persuade the other that their way of relating is 'wrong' and that 'you should be relating more like me'. Many couples are comprised of one dissonant and one consonant type, and the edginess of their different ways of doing things can create great chemistry and a balance of both gentle warmth and fieriness, or it can descend into a situation where both people have feelings of loneliness and alienation.

If a couple share a dissonant contact style in a relationship, both people might enjoy debate, argument and being competitive with each other, whilst both may also enjoy time apart, choosing to maintain a lot of individual tasks and interests. There are positives to this, but it can also lead to the relationship being too separate, with insufficient sharing of harmonious and loving feelings, leaving the relational space somewhat arid and fractious. If both people in a couple share a consonant contact style, the relationship may feel harmonious and companionable, but this can lead to a platonic, familial feeling which lacks the edginess necessary for passionate engagement.

Dissonant types in groups

Similar dynamics are created within work groups, friendship groups, family groups and training groups. As a trainer, it is easy to see the practitioner students who are dissonant right off the bat; they may express cynical feelings about the training topic or personal feelings of wishing they were somewhere else other than the training group. In fact, just being in a group can feel uncomfortable for them due to the pressures of having to 'fit in'.

These participants may predominantly query, challenge, and disagree with the material presented, bringing new perspectives and fresh ideas into the room. Alternatively, dissonant types might express their differentiation by not bringing themselves in much at all, appearing a bit disengaged, ambivalent or on the edge of the group.

There are many signals from these people that highlight the differences between themselves and others, and it is important to offer contact that is strong enough to respect and reflect the traction that they are seeking. Once that is offered, these participants often turn into the most engaged and insightful members of the group. However, if a trainer interprets their way of engaging as 'negative' in some way and therefore subtly avoids them, shames them, or placates them, thereby providing a contact boundary that is either overbearing or too fragile, then these participants can become disgruntled, disinterested, bored and absent.

These learning points are also important for therapists working with couples, who may find the dissonant member of a couple to be hard to reach, perhaps concluding that they are 'being resistant', rather than recognizing that they are joining in with a different relational style.

Consonant types in groups

Within groups, participants who are consonant in style often make good eye contact, nod their heads to material that is presented, feedback what is useful about the material, and join in with experiential work in a way that creates mutual ground with other participants.

Confluent participants might suffer from being overshadowed by others, feeling shy and afraid to speak up with questions. As trainers, it is understandable that despite whatever contact style we ourselves possess, if we are nervous and seeking validation from the group in order to reassure ourselves, we will likely have a preference for the confluent group members' way of relating to us and subtly focus more on them. We may even feel protective towards them if there are highly verbal dissonant group members who are dominating the space.

Balancing the types

It is therefore extremely important to give equal amounts of attention to each participant in a group or a couple. This may involve encouraging consonant types to critique or question the teaching material, whilst encouraging dissonant types to notice what is working well for them, as well as debating what is not. This way of working, which maps contact styles, both supports a person's chosen way of doing things, as well as helping them over the edge into more of the unfamiliar end of that polarity.

Contact boundaries and empathy

As therapists, our capacity to notice the contact that is being constructed in the therapeutic space – and our ability to meet that contact with a mirroring capacity that is matched energetically and verbally – is essential to the work. Empathy is a central plank of most therapeutic approaches, and it is important for us to consider what empathy means in terms of empathizing with the psychological landscape at any given moment. Many practitioners will say that empathy for the client is a form of experiential contact with what the client is feeling, a compassionate resonance with the client.

If we broaden empathy to include the overall map of a client, couple or group's landscape, including conscious 'me' and unconscious 'not me' territory, then empathy expands to the overall dynamic and the energy that it is taking to manage the resulting tension at the edge. If, as therapists, we are not going to take sides in our client's internal conflicts, then we must have empathy towards the conflict as a whole, whilst being able to relate to, and move between, what is valid and meaningful on both sides of the edge.

Empathy such as this is expressed most effectively through the type of contact boundary that we establish with clients, and how able we are to shift our contact style to reflect the nature of the material that is emerging and coming to the fore. As a client's material changes in its quality, so must our contact boundary within the relationship.

Maintaining contact with what is foreground requires that a therapist be able to increase or decrease intensity in the strength of traction, assertiveness, softness, warmth, vulnerability, clarity, incisiveness, intuitiveness, pragmatism, realism, creativity, silence, receptivity, articulation and so on, as foreground material changes and fluctuates.

Creating mirroring contact boundaries

- If a client presents at any time during therapy with a sarcastic, patronizing tone of voice, or with high levels of subtle or explicit disagreement with your therapeutic interventions, these are signals that there may be conflict brewing with unconscious content that might include powerful, challenging, pioneering and unpredictable material. Instead of responding to these signals as signs of defensiveness, it is more useful to increase your own energy levels in the room as therapist. This might mean becoming more alert, making your interventions shorter and more direct; naming and describing the quality of what seems to be emerging in the room.

  If, instead of mirroring the contact style, the therapist remains apparently 'unchanged', retaining a soft tone of voice and questioning the client in terms of what is going on, then the client is likely to become agitated and escalated because their contact style in that moment is not being met and mirrored.

  Mirroring requires therapists to meet and match the energy of what is emerging whilst also noticing, naming, and describing what is occurring, which helps to create a sense of relationality.

- If a client is direct with you, then incorporate directness into your guiding style. If a client is in a reflective space, become more reflective yourself whilst naming and describing the quality of reflectiveness in the space. If a client is quiet and pensive, bring low-key qualities into your interventions and energy. Remember the archetypal work in the last chapter and seek to embody the essential transpersonal qualities in the client's contact style, rather than simply mimicking their behaviour.

- Overly questioning a client can generate feelings of being interrogated, provoking defensive, aggressive and vulnerable responses. Being excessively analytic or interpretive of a client's presentation can also activate their defences if they feel that you are accusing them of something, criticizing or making them 'wrong', even though that might not have been your intention.

  A way forward that does not assign blame for an emerging process (particularly a conflict) is to 'third party it' by commenting on the space between you. This means sharing what you are experiencing in the space between you at any given moment.

  Rather than making 'you' or 'I' statements, we can turn to 'we,' 'us' and 'the space between us' statements. This might sound like 'there seems to be some spikiness in the room today,' or 'it seems important to really notice the differences between us today,' or 'there's an urgency to find solutions and answer questions today,' and so on.

  The therapy world places a lot of emphasis on clients making 'I' statements to encourage them to take ownership of what they are thinking, feeling, or doing, and there are times when this is valuable. However, field theory reminds us that field phenomena is not something that we can cut into pieces of 'what belongs to whom' and it can be counterproductive for the therapist to appear in a superior position, as if they are not part of the dynamic by speaking in terms of 'what you (the client) are doing, defending against, or avoiding'. Instead, if therapists acknowledge that the process is shared, using 'we', 'our space', 'here between us today' statements, a democracy is established that allows the therapist to be more interactive and the client to feel 'joined'.

Interruption to contact

As we improve our capacity to maintain a contact boundary with the ever-changing qualities within the client's process, we are better able to notice when contact is interrupted or severed. These interruptions are often an indication that the client or the therapeutic relationship itself has reached an edge and that edge figures' defences have 'severed the phone line' to prevent unconscious material that is deemed as dangerous from entering the relational field of awareness.

These moments can be punctuated by either therapist or client unexpectedly changing the subject: dissociating, getting defensive, losing track of what is going on in the room, unusual physical signals, or a noticeable drop of energy in the room are all possible signals that contact with a process may have been interrupted or severed.

As with the work of maintaining a contact boundary, if it seems that contact with the process has been severed, practice noticing and describing what is going on such as: 'it seems as if something has cut across what we were exploring' or 'it feels like we've lost contact with where we were going together'.

Pause and hang around the moment of severing, rather than just letting things run on as if nothing has happened, with the intention of inquiring into what was happening at the moment of interruption and what sort of edge you might have been on together that provoked the interruption. If a therapist doesn't let a client know that they have noticed such interruptions, the client may feel that the therapist is not paying attention; leaving them feeling disappointed that they have been able to divert away from something meaningful without the therapist noticing.

The increasing gains for a client working with a therapist who can maintain good contact boundaries that are flexible and responsive, is the client's internalizing of that capacity. This potentially allows the client to maintain good contact with their own internal experience, reducing tendencies to break contact when emotional and psychological material arises that they have edges against. As a client strengthens their capacity to be contactful with the variations occurring in their internal landscapes, their cohesiveness strengthens and their internal leadership increases. This development of an internal leader that is flexible yet constant, strong yet fluid, direct yet compassionate, can be one of the single most important tasks of therapy.

Focused leadership within the psyche

I could dress up the term 'focused leadership' with clinical language that refers to the I-Self connection and development of that connection through the two main archetypes of transpersonal Will and Love, but for the sake of using everyday language that as practitioners we can immediately use with clients in a way that they (and we) understand, I will stick to the word 'leadership'.

Many of the presenting issues and psychopathology that we face as clinicians are rooted in a client's lack of psychological leadership. With multiplicity circulating within us, a lack of leadership is an anxiety creating, panic inducing and fragmenting experience. Internal leadership is something that we can develop through the way in which we make contact with our experience: the way in which we attend to and listen to ourselves, the way that we are able to construct, move and maintain effective boundaries with internal material that is not useful in any given moment, and the capacity that we have for sustained focus on both our external world and our internal reality.

To help the concept of internal leadership to become more alive and concrete, we can compare our internal worlds to political regimes. Without a democratic system of governance whereby leaders are elected, a country can be vulnerable to dictatorship or military leadership. Psychologically this is the same as policing edge figures exerting powerful control over conscious and unconscious forces. Conversely, in the same scenario, a lack of elected leadership can lead to civil uprising and conflict, or even civil war. This is reflected in psyches that have weak edge figures who are unable to create psychological order, leading to a descent into internal civil war between conflicting, competing psychological content, creating fragmentation. If there are no effective internal boundaries in place, there will be a weak sense of identity and a low capacity to distinguish between reality and delusion; this sort of psychological chaos creates heightened anxiety and paranoia, potentially leading to psychotic states.

Both outcomes are a result of a lack of leadership, and they highlight the necessity for creating an internally democratic attitude towards the multiplicity within ourselves, and for the need to continually 'elect', through acts of will-oriented choice, internal leadership that reflects our values and principles.

Psychological dictatorship

Psychological dictatorship regimes create a harsh, punitive experience of life for someone, even if their external reality is relatively comfortable, because no matter what good things come to that person, everything is filtered through a meaning making regime that dictates and controls the level of aliveness. As is the case with such political regimes, the truth is a murky reality – honesty is suppressed and freedom from the regime must be found through covert, secretive means: appearing to follow the regime rules for fear of punishment, disallowing spontaneity and creativity, and perpetuating fearful, paranoid atmospheres.

It can be extremely hard to work with clients who possess these sorts of psychological regimes as they often keep secrets from the therapist, fearing that if they tell the truth that it will be used against them in some way. This can lead to a coded form of signalling to the therapist of how they really feel, which can be frustrating for both client and therapist. The most useful way forward is for the therapist to pick up on the policed, tightly controlled, ominous atmosphere that is conjured in the room with these clients, working immanently with an almost forensic reality check ing of what a client really means within the code being offered.

In these cases, it is vital that the therapist clearly communicates the meaning they are making from what the client is telling them and checking out if that is what the client intended to convey, or whether there are alternative, deeper meanings that are too risky to share directly. Even if the client says that there are other meanings that they don't feel safe disclosing, the very fact that the secret content has been acknowledged helps to alleviate the tension and paranoia in the space, bringing the relationship to more honest ground. What matters is that the prevailing process structure that is controlling the meaning making landscape is identified, shared, and explored.

As these clients begin to develop the ability to notice and describe what is occurring for them in their internal regime, they can begin to sow the seeds of creating an alternative leadership that, when more fully formed, will begin to challenge the policing rulership. Learning to describe what is occurring, what is forbidden and why, and practising making small changes to the level of permission they give themselves to reveal what is important – all allow step-by-step gains to be made.

Psychological civil war

Fragmented psychological regimes, where civil war has erupted due to an absence of rulership structures, can also feel dangerous in the countertransference of the therapist. This kind of danger comes not from the punishment of breaking the rules, but from the chaotic explosions and lack of cohesiveness that such clients experience. They can veer from feeling needy and desperate to aloof and critical. Insightful dialogue that a therapist might think has gone well during a session may, to their surprise, be criticized by the client the next time they see them. Consequently, 'meaning making' shifts unpredictability, with an atmosphere of feeling at sea, subject to erratic weather conditions.

Developing a compass within the therapeutic relationship is vital in helping to acknowledge the internal experience that these clients are having. In similarity with working on dictatorship regimes, the therapist must work immanently in the here and now, bringing a phenomenological perspective to what is occurring in the space between therapist and client, inquiring into the meaning that is being made at any given moment to try and create mutual ground to stand on together. This creates a compass which can identify and map moments of corroborated understanding, as a reality check of what is 'due north' in the client's psyche.

Allowing many moments of disagreement in the service of knowing what the client is really meaning and experiencing, will involve the therapist offering meaning making statements, giving the client delineated material to correct or alter. This forms the client's capacity to track their own process and, once tracking and narrating develops, seeds of internal leadership structures are sown from the experience of 'I am here, and I know that I am here because I can track where I am and narrate it to myself and to you'. For clients with no leadership, this capacity to track themselves leads to a stronger outline of 'who I am' and defines the edge between their conscious 'me' and unconscious 'not me', which is vital for an increasing experience of cohesiveness.

Leadership and existential anxiety

With strong internal leadership, there is a sense that somebody is 'at home' internally, providing an internal narrative that contains evidence-based reality (rather than fantasy, projection and assumption), and who 'talks to us' in firm but compassionate ways that reach beyond our survival, towards our potential to thrive. If we can develop leadership such as this, we deal with the different parts of ourselves with a steady hand, feeling that we have an ally who is on our side yet who will also tell us the truth about ourselves.

This provides an on-going feeling of 'I am here' cohesiveness that is grounding, relational and trustworthy. Such cohesiveness allows us to handle the variations of life, which by its very nature is not always trustworthy, as circumstances can be disappointing and people can let us down as well as love us. To be able to maintain a sense of well being in the face of life's variations we must develop a capacity for internal continuity, rather than using manipulative, coercive ways of trying to force our external world to stay constant for us, which will always be a losing battle.

I have noticed that, with the increase in anxiety disorders in the consulting room, there has been a concurrent increase in self-help and spiritual approaches that offer 'you can create your own reality' approaches. Rather than calming a rising tide of anxiety, these approaches seem to have contributed to its escalation through raising expectations that we can have it all if we only believe enough that we can. I have worked with many people who have interpreted these 'create your own reality' approaches as a spiritual supermarket – believing that if their home and work lives are not going the way they want, that they must be failing in the task to get the products of experience that they wish for.

My experience is that it is incredibly important to have a sense of there being something larger than ourselves in the world, that is beyond our control, if we are to avoid developing omnipotent fantasies of our capacity as human beings. Accepting that there is an existential reality that is beyond our ability to manipulate or in any way avoid, is extremely important. As therapists it is our job at times to deliver the bad news to clients that we can't guarantee that their lives are going to be 'ok' in terms of the outcomes that they want: that they will never get sick, lose loved ones, avoid accidents, or in any other way get a free pass from the inevitable challenges that we all face.

Far from escalating anxiety, this truth telling of evidenced fact that humanness brings with it an essential uncertainty, is sometimes met with anger but also with relief by clients. Facing the possibility that 'no rescue is coming' from a powerful source – who will give them preferential treatment if they behave appropriately – creates more real ground to stand on. What seems to be the cause of this relief is that anxiety is no longer lodged in pathological grandiosity that our safety lies solely in our own hands, but instead it can be viewed as a distress signal from the psyche which senses that we are deluding ourselves about the nature of reality.

However grandiose we become, the survival part of our brain knows full well that the world is unpredictable. If we can accept reality as it is, rather than replacing it with our preferred fantasy of how we would like it to be, thereby relaxing the obsessive-compulsive rituals that are our weaponry against the unpredictability of potential pain, then we can get on with the task of facing these variations and the intelligent existential anxiety that comes with it.

This moves us to what is possible for us to take charge of: our inner landscapes and the dynamics that populate them. For most of us, having a strong, reliable, resourceful, supportive, honest person that we look up to – who would be by our side if our lives hit the skids – would go a long way towards helping us feel safer in the knowledge that difficult days may come. Developing allying internal leadership is a way of creating that sense of not being alone during challenging times, reliably there for us, through thick and thin. Having supportive friendships and family is important, but our psyches know that those people might not be available when we need them the most, and that there is a limit to what we can expect from others.

The truth is that our unconscious worlds are extremely clued up, with a keen sense of the realities of life; this is why we create edges to that 'knowingness', because it can frighten us. Such instinctive wisdom is an incredible resource that, if we start to trust rather than split off, has the potential to become the anchored ground that we draw strength from, lean into, and place our faith in. As is highlighted in previous chapters, the unconscious is not just full of pathology and wounding, it is also full of existential truth, and instinctive knowledge. When we barricade ourselves off from the feelings that we don't want to experience, we also barricade off the wisdom which has the potential to give us a trustworthy capacity to cope with what life brings us.

Ways of actively developing leadership in the psyche

- Ask a client to think about a historical or current-day leader that they are inspired by and invite the client to describe that person in as much detail as possible; this detail may be largely a fantasy of what the person is like, rather than based on fact. Given that this is about building ideas about the type of leadership that inspires them, it is ok to work with projections, as long as those projections are mined for details of what matters to the client about the leaders that they feel drawn to, with as much of a realistic, humanizing slant as possible.

In other words, mapping leadership with a client requires material that is as rounded as possible, consisting of qualities at both ends of polarities, in order that they do not use this exercise to simply construct new edges with forbidden ways of being. Good leaders are vulnerable as well as strong, they are confident as well as having moments of doubt, they are listeners who are also out-spoken, they are reflective but spontaneous when the need arises, they are kind but might have to be ruthless at times.

Look at ways that the client is already demonstrating those leadership qualities internally within themselves and externally in their lives, and find strategies for connecting more fully to the areas that they are not so developed in.

- Facilitate the client to develop a self-talk that is evidence-based and encouraging of getting reality-checks about events or situations that they are not sure about, instead of building fantasy narratives that are based on defensive fears and assumptions. Self-talk that is descriptive, encouraging, and capable of naming reality is vastly different from the type of internal commentary that goes on for many people. An internal commentator is usually a fantasist: judgemental, pompous, punitive, controlling, shaming and analytically punishing.

Internal commentary is often described as a superego or critical subpersonality, which does not go nearly far enough in terms of addressing the all-encompassing consequences of an ever-present commentator who is employed by edge figures to keep a client under control. The commentator is not just a part of us, it is an encompassing, relentless, ever-present attitude towards our experience with an aim to constantly nag, doubt, and shame us into 'staying within the lines of acceptability'. This crippling commentary will continue until it is replaced with a consistent narrative that is describing rather than analyzing, compassionate rather than punitive, realistic rather than fantasizing, and effective rather than disabling.

Developing internal leadership that can narrate our experience – supporting us to face reality as it is, rather than undermining us – is achieved through the repetition of practise. Sometimes it is sufficient to do this internally, but at the beginning it is worth suggesting that clients practice by speaking aloud to themselves, because that can produce the same calming effects as hearing another person speaking to us in strong, insightful ways.

- Suggest that the client starts the day with an internal 'touching base' with themselves; assessing what tasks, needs and challenges might be coming up and consciously choosing the qualities that the client wants to encourage in their own internal landscapes. They are 'being their own leader' when they set the agenda for what is realistic, manageable or even desirable, allocating to other defined days tasks which are unrealistic in terms of being achievable that day.

- Days can also be ended with internal de-briefs of how the day has gone, highlighting what has been most meaningful for them, giving appreciation to themselves and others for those moments. It is also useful to notice what has disturbed them, with accurate describing of what led up to the disturbing event, what about the event itself was uncomfortable, and which dilemmas they might have been left with – which is not the same as resolving the disturbing event, ranting about it, or being consumed by it.

Good leadership notices when we are best placed to deal with things that are troubling us, rather than resorting to denial or obsessiveness which goes over and over what is troubling, usually with no resolution. The main purpose of these de-briefs is to attend to our own experience in a direct manner that is a straightforward, un-flinching reality checking rather than fantasy-based, and which is compassionate about what is troubling.

- Encourage clients to spend time with people who they respect as having healthy leadership qualities. If it's possible to include working for someone that they respect, that's great, but it can also include attending lectures or presentations by people they admire, reading autobiographies, watching documentaries of people who lead in certain fields, as well as cultivating friendships with those who possess leadership qualities that they value. As therapists, if we have developed our own leadership capacity, we are also potentially potent role models in our work with others, and clients might describe 'hearing your voice in my head' as they internalize our way of speaking, narrating and being contactful with their material.

- Support clients to progress in their home and work environments: to consider taking on responsibility, becoming more direct rather than avoiding potential difficulties, being collegial yet also putting forward their own ideas, and developing the capacity to tolerate criticism through internal allying of themselves, which gives them more scope to take risks.

Internal regimes that encourage good decision-making

If we possess internal dictatorships, then the dictator, military head of state, or committee of senior officers makes the decisions, and the collective must adhere to it without having a say. If we are experiencing internal anarchy due to a collapse of psychological governance, decisions are not made, because the process of deciding is constantly highjacked by the collective's turmoil, creating a situation where decisions are endlessly argued over. If we have developed an internal democracy where many parts of us get to vote, then there will be a majority decision where at least 51% will get the outcome that they voted for and 49% will have to live with it.

Whilst not being ideal in terms of collective satisfaction, internal democracy is the closest we can come to being able to make decisions that give our psychological collectives a vote, even if not everybody will like the outcome. The two alternative regimes – dictatorships and consensus collectives – both paralyze decision making, with a dictatorship leading to violence in the psyche and potential revolution, whereas in consensus regimes everybody must get on side for a decision to be validated, which is too time consuming to be realistic.

Real world collectives who use a consensus decision-making format can spend weeks or months deciding on the colour of a new rug, let alone decisions about more meaningful matters. This is a useful structure if you have a small group which is interested in using decision making to explore power in the group, or as an example of unfolding different roles in the group dynamic. However, for the scale and number of decisions that need to be made within the political governance of a client's psychological landscape, a hierarchy that gives the internal collective some say in decisions, without being held hostage by the endless 'yes buts' that manifest, is essential in terms of developing an ability to be decisive.

I am constantly surprised by the number of clients whose presenting issues are not directly related to decision-making, but through the course of therapy it emerges that they are severely incapacitated in their ability to be decisive. A client who is unable to make decisions in relation to the small and larger aspects of their lives is likely to feel frustrated, resentful, disempowered, anxious and depressed. This incapacity is often due to:

- A belief that they need to create a 100% consensus internally where every part of them agrees with the decision for fear that it could be 'the wrong one'. This idealism is often based on a superstitious feeling that any variation in certainty is a sign that they are doing the wrong thing.

  This belief must be challenged in therapy, with an inquiry into the client's rationalization for such a belief and exploring the possibility that expecting a 100% consensus psychologically is not realistic, given our multiplicity. Clients benefit from knowing that internal leadership which takes a majority decision based on 'more of me is leaning towards A, rather than B' is fine, if ongoing feedback of how that decision rolls out is taken into consideration. The permission to change our minds is key if our feedback is that the original decision has not brought about the expected outcome, in which case the decision can be re-decided upon and changed accordingly.

- A belief that all decisions are unchangeable and therefore must be 'forever right' leads to an unchanging psychological status quo, with prevailing norms that must never be deviated from. Pointing out to clients that decisions need to change over time to stay valid can often be a radical realization, if they have previously perceived the only good decision to be a life-long one.

- The earlier two points can all be part of a client's fear of being punished or held accountable as a failure, if their decisions do not yield the result that they want. Fear of humiliation and shame if a decision does not work out as planned is a major reason why people are not decisive. Other people's opinions matter more than their own potential to live a dynamic life and it is effective for therapy to focus on the importance of clients' own satisfaction and fulfilment being paramount over and above the opinions of others.

  I have oftentimes told clients that the human psyche is made up of a mixture of criticism as well as support of ourselves and others and therefore hoping to derive a totally positive response from others is a fruitless task. Whilst being a bit of a shock, most clients find this honest appraisal of human nature a relief, before getting down to the important task of earning their own self-respect by being decisive and creating a more dynamic life for themselves.

People who lead effective, dynamic lives take a lot of risks through decisive action in one direction and then they roll with the punches and feedback loops as to whether to veer left or right once they have set a ball in motion. Life appears to respond to action-oriented people, who throw stones in the lake and then follow the ripples, rather than sitting on the bank and waiting to feel sure about where the ripples will go. Therapy can also suffer with 'paralysis by analysis', with its overly reflective bias rooted in belief that the more aware we are, the more likely we are to make decisions that are 'right' from the get go.

Time and again I have witnessed clients feeling more expressive, creative, liberated and alive when they begin to take action from their 51% hunch that one direction is more of interest to them than another, with full permission to change direction if necessary. The more we interact with life by interfacing with it in a dynamic way, the more feedback we get, and the more feedback we get the wiser we become.

Therapy that subtly suggests clients should keep themselves overly safe, – not taking risks 'just in case', emphasizing self-care in a way that leans on clients' self-doubt and fear – does not teach clients to be more effective decision makers in their own lives. As a reflective profession, many practitioners have a strong bias towards being thoughtful, which is indeed an extremely important element of therapy. However, when clients need support to become activated, therapists might hold back out of concern for the client or a fear of being blamed by the client if decisiveness is followed and outcomes are not as wished. During these times we practitioners benefit from looking at our approach to decisiveness in our own lives.

Decisiveness often makes somebody magnetic; it also dramatically increases their feedback from the world, creating a sort of energy generator that builds upon itself. Consequently, people are drawn to those who practice decisiveness, but such magnetism can also attract envious attacks or caution and doubt from friends and family who offer 'do you really think that's a good idea'. The answer is that we can never know if something is a good idea, even if we have run probabilities about likely outcomes. All we can ever truthfully say is that it is the most attractive idea to us, right here and now, despite fears and misgivings, and if we lean into that action we will bend with the feedback.

Becoming co-creative with life is a fulfilling path, through developing internal leadership that we can trust to stand by us as we say 'yes' to one route at a fork in the road, knowing full well that at some later date we may have to change our mind as alternative routes present themselves. I often witness clients increasing their courage to take action, building on the evidential feedback that such decisiveness brings them, generating a stronger sense of self with greater self-respect. A good balance between risk taking and maintenance, and the contact that comes with feedback loops, enhances someone's experience of relating to life.

Generating healthy internal governance and leadership that can make decisions, change direction depending on the weather conditions and circumstances without recrimination, with the capacity to listen to feedback loops and learn from them, is a wonderful outcome of good therapy. Given that generating leadership requires a capacity to become more straightforward, self-allying, decisive, and visible, it may well be that a client must face conflict from others who may feel threatened, defensive and aggressive towards those gains. Good leaders do not just sit on the fence, in an endless round of hedging their bets and diplomacy; they seek to be direct and honest with their values, and receptively open with their thinking. Therefore, the capacity to enter a conflictual relational space, should it arise, is necessary.

Hunting process; the capacity to develop good contact through conflict

The capacity to teach clients healthy approaches to relationally based conflict, in a way that deepens intimacy and good contact, requires us as therapists to also develop that capacity in ourselves. Trainers, couple therapists, individual therapists, family therapists and supervisors all benefit from developing an ability to head into potentially conflictual dynamics. Having taught many groups on this topic, most participants admit that they find conflict intimidating and that they fear things getting out of control.

The capacity to stay focused on what is going on psychodynamically when our own emotions are heating up is challenging, and it makes sense that our physiology prepares with fight or flight responses when conflict is in the consulting or training room. Practising an ability to notice the early signals of conflict, in order to unfold them, is essential if we are to provide the necessary contact with these intense processes.

Learning the way in which our bodies are primed to set off a cascade of physiological changes when we feel afraid or threatened in some way, is the first step towards accepting that these changes are not a sign that something is wrong, rather that something significant is occurring that needs attention and contact. Most of us interpret fight or flight responses internally as a sign to 'flee' – physically, emotionally, or cognitively – from whatever we interpret to be the origin of the threat.

This fear reaction is totally normal; the prickling of sweat in the armpits, flush to the face, increased tension in our muscles and slight feeling of anxiety that arises with an increased heart rate, are commonplace when another person shows implicit or explicit criticism or challenges us – with the accompanying feelings of shame, humiliation and irritation that are internally provoked in response.

Learning to head towards provocative signals may be counterintuitive, but it is one of the most powerful ways to hunt meaningful processes. I am bolding this statement because it is one of the most useful changes that a therapist can make to their way of working. As essential organs and muscles are prioritized by increased blood flow during a fight or flight response, our brains receive less blood supply, affecting our capacity to think. Our ability to be articulate drops, so we must make shorter interventions, naming the atmosphere without understanding why the provocation is present. This involves noticing our avoidance when it kicks in, so that we may begin to hunt for what is really going on and to encourage it to become explicit and relational, rather than implicit and evasive.

Physiological responses to fear

Physiologically, when we feel afraid, the following physical reactions occur before we are even aware cognitively of what is going on:

- The hypothalamus activates the sympathetic nervous system and the adrenal-cortical system, which speed the body up, creating muscle tension and alertness.

- Glands and muscles are primed for action and the hormones adrenalin and noradrenalin are released into the bloodstream, which increase our heart rate and blood pressure.

- The adrenal cortex is signalled to release approximately thirty hormones that prepare the body to face the threat it perceives to be present.

- Along with increased muscle tension, heart rate and bloody pressure, our pupils dilate to increase our capacity to see clearly, blood-glucose increases, the hair stands up on our skin, and veins constrict as blood is diverted away from the skin to provide increased blood to major muscle groups, creating a chilly feeling. Most importantly, the brain is primed to focus on the big picture, rather than small tasks.

These responses do not just occur when we feel provoked or threatened, they can occur when we walk into any sort of new situation – if something feels 'out of place' in some way, if we are meeting new people, or we are required to perform. Couples who come for therapy are often locked into a continual fight or flight mode, leading to chronic defensive-aggressive dynamics, as is sometimes the case with organizations, families and anyone who works front line with the public (this includes therapeutic practitioners).

Beginning to recognize these sensations – feeling chills, increased heart rate, a flush of physical alertness along with a drop in cognitive capacity – is vital if we are to ready ourselves to stay focused and to start moving towards uncomfortable processes. Choosing to divert away through silence, placating, confluence or flattery will shut potential conflicts down until they emerge at another time.

The risks of avoiding conflict

Such avoidance may be interpreted by the other person as evidence that we can't cope, which is not the sort of message that therapists consciously wish to send to clients. Sometimes a therapist can become disapproving, superior, or patronizing when they feel criticized or challenged by clients or training groups. The therapist may assume that it is the client's defences that are in operation, rather than a challenge to engage in a more intense and direct way. The client may consequently feel that being assertive, challenging or critical is not emotionally or psychologically acceptable to their therapist.

Such reactions from therapists sends challenging signals underground, eventually leading to the client terminating therapy or reverting to passive-aggressive ways of asserting themselves in the room. Therapists are often concerned that if they notice and attend to potential conflict that it will pour petrol on the fire and provoke it further. However, when provocative signals are noticed and acknowledged they often ease and expand into a deeper story, whereas ignoring such signals can conversely aggravate them further.

If a practitioner feels alarmed that they are physically at risk in some way during work with a client, then it is vital that they explicitly name that the atmosphere feels threatening, and that unless the threat reduces then the session will end. Putting down firm boundaries that reminds the client of what the therapist will work with and will not work with is essential at this point. Repetitive assertiveness, rather than passive avoidance, is still the most effective way to work if a therapist is afraid for their safety. Firm statements that 'we are going to stop this escalation so that the session can continue, and if that is not possible then we will end the session early today' are effective, as statements create boundaries which are often calming.

This way of containing a feeling of potential violence in the room is also effective with couple therapy and in training groups. It is worth pointing out that prematurely ending sessions is a last resort, and that once an escalation has been halted, if there is the possibility to think about what was provocative from a calmer place, then that is preferential.

During heightened tension, noticing the physiological heightening in our bodies is the first step in steadying ourselves and beginning to ask ourselves what was said or done that raised our hackles. Pausing the work and bringing attention to a remark that might have been the cause of our physical reaction is a useful place to start, even though we don't know where that will lead us. We then have the possibility of heading into the unknown with an inquiry that starts to excavate what may be lying beneath a comment, tone of voice, physical signal or simply a sense of something being 'off'. Sometimes this happens because we ourselves say something provocative to the client, and it is just as important to inquire into that feeling and bring attention to 'what might be occurring between us? It seems as if we are going in circles and I am wondering what might be difficult to see, say or do?'

If a client directly accuses you of something, or expresses anger or criticism, it is important to slow things down and inquire into the kernel of truth in the criticism, whilst also staying with the responses that are evoked in you. You may feel wobbly because of the fight-or-flight responses in your body but that is ok, keep going anyway, even though you may feel inarticulate, embarrassed and unsure. You are both on an edge together and it is important to ask yourself 'what edge are we on right now, what is difficult to face? What archetype might be edgy to experience and express? What is over this edge that I am afraid of?' Find ways to work with the 'us' and 'we' of the moment, referencing the third space between you rather than getting into 'you over there' and 'me over here' stand offs. Remember that something in the field of your relationship is filling with a shared dynamic that has importance for you both to stay with.

Ways of working with conflict

- Notice a heightened fight or flight response in your physical state.

- Turn your attention inwards and take a few deeper breaths and try to relax your muscles a little.

- Re-run the last couple of interventions, and pinpoint what was said that raised your hackles.

- Ask yourself: what is it about my client's signals that I find provocative? What landscape do I see us in right now? What is occurring in this landscape, what conflict is brewing? What matters most that is coming fore-ground?

- Sit up in your chair, give direct eye contact, and tell the client that it seems that something important is going on right now, that you don't know exactly what it is, but you wish to pause and attend to what is happening. Check out with the client what they are noticing.

- If you are able, describe the atmosphere in the room, and the imaginal sense that you have of the landscape you are in together and what is occurring. Check out with the client how they are receiving your images.

- If the client picks up the ball that you have thrown to them, keep the dialogue going, unfolding the dynamic as much as possible, using 'third party' use of the space between you rather than subtly attributing blame and keeping the dialogue relational.

- The journey of unfolding conflictual situations with clients is that you may discover that both of you are ner-vously touching into deeper, more honest territory. These explorations often lead to a deepening of intimacy and trust between you and it's important to appreciate the client for having the courage to stay with tense dialogues.

- If the client does not pick up the ball that you throw to them, but lets it drop at their feet, giving you a nonchalant stare and shrugging their shoulders as if they don't know what you are talking about, don't be put off. Ask 'how is it for you that I am sensing something prickly between us, while you do not?' Stay with the client's insistence that 'nothing is wrong' and explore what is it is like for both of you to have different experiences of what is between you in that moment.

- Ask the client how they differ in their perception of what is occurring and invite them to expand on their sense of things and compare the similarities and differences. The main point is to stay firm in the position that both of your perceptions and experiences are valid, and therefore a part of the puzzle, even if they are different pieces in that given moment.

- Unfolding difficult material with clients who avoid your attempts to make tension explicit, or who deny that tension is present, may simply lead to an acknowledgement that differences of perception are ok, and you can suggest that something might be brewing that is still unconscious, but which may bubble up later on, suggesting that the client notice if these themes emerge between the current session and the next time that you will meet.

- When working with couples, the same principles apply, except that you are treating the couple as having their own 'units of work' and therefore you can make similar interventions to those outlined in the previous bullet points, except that you will be inviting each member of the couple to respond to your sense that something is brewing in the room.

- When working with groups, you can do some one-to-one work with a participant who is being provocative with you, using the interventions outlined above and then open it to the whole group to hear their responses. If there is a conflict between two of the course participants, you can work in the same way that you would during a couple session and then open it to the larger group for their responses, thoughts and experiences.

If the whole group seems to be engaged in a conflict you can work with it by initially naming that there seems to a disagreement emerging, describing the landscape that you sense the group to be in and inviting them to each individually share their own sense of the landscape of the group at that time, which could then be explored. Alternatively, you can dive straight into the conflict, bypassing symbolic inquiry, and ask each person to share their experience of what is brewing in the group.

If you want to do some field theory work on what is constellating you can ask people who seem to be sharing similar 'roles' within the field to cluster together and help each other explore the roles that connect them: the values, meaning, significance of what is being experienced within their own cluster. Next, encourage each cluster to share their explorations with the other clusters, with a willingness to really receive other cluster's points of view. The therapist can circulate between each cluster and support them to clarify the depth of what they are experiencing and standing for – taking care to support each cluster equally to fully state their experience.

The aim of working in this way is that no one person has to take responsibility for a group role, and this is particularly useful if one or two participants are being criticized by the rest of the group. Splitting the group into clusters in this way flattens the playing field and gives everybody support to express what is important, making it easier to listen to and acknowledge the positions of the other clusters. The purpose is not to reach a resolution, but that each cluster fully expresses their own position and fully acknowledges the other clusters.

Appreciate everybody in the group for staying with the heightened experience and don't be afraid to bring in teaching points once the conflict has been explored, to share your growing knowledge of how to work with conflict as a road to intimacy, and to apply what has emerged to the teaching material that you were engaged with when the conflict emerged in the group.

Remember to work with edges, describing landscape and archetypal characters that seem to be present in the field of a conflict. We can constantly utilize the imaginal space to bring illumination to conflictual situations where we feel stuck, scared, blank and metaphorically pinned to the wall. Symbolic use of the imaginal space can offer keys which open doors to unconscious material that is fighting its way into the field of awareness in a relationship. Rather than taking it personally, bring your capacity to imagine what is emerging in the space as a whole, avoiding the creation of trenches between warring factions with their own versions of the truth. Conflicts are ultimately more about what connects us than divides us.

During conflicts we all utilize avoidance mechanisms and the common ones that are used during conflicts are:

- Avoiding the issue through denial, pretending that nothing is going on, feigning ignorance of provocative comments, claiming that the comment was a joke, or accusing the other person of 'reading too much into the situation'.

- Deflecting by 'throwing a bone' in another direction to put the other person off the scent or using distraction techniques by changing the subject.

- Using attack as the best form of defence. This may be a counter attack aimed at causing confusion, or it may be utilizing emotional expression that is designed to defuse the situation and distract from the conflict.

When emotions become heightened in this way, it is important to suggest that you both slow things down so that nothing important gets missed; be understanding of the emotion being expressed, whilst also suggesting that something significant is occurring that may be causing discomfort.

- Going unconscious through feeling sleepy, forgetting what has just happened, rationalizing it away, or deciding there is not enough time to 'properly attend' to what is occurring.

- Glossing over what is happening through banter, jokes, or aggressive energy towards safer targets such as third parties who aren't present or external events, to diffuse attention away from the conflict itself.

- Finding an excuse to leave the room just as tensions are rising, such as to go to the toilet, or answer the phone.

This is by no means an exhaustive list of the ways in which we de-rail conflicts rather than deal with them. The key is to be understanding of why it feels difficult to look at what is happening, whilst also stating the importance of dealing with conflictual material when it arises, so that that it can properly attended to in a way that leaves everyone 'intact'.

I cannot stress enough that if conflict is left unattended in the consulting room, it can lead to an assumption that the client is 'too much' for the therapist; as a result, taboo territory is created which degrades the potency of the therapeutic space and leaves everyone dissatisfied. If we remove the assumption that all conflict is dangerous, and instead see it as a form of contact that is just as relevant as any other – especially in its capacity to create aliveness, honesty and intimacy in a relationship that may be more trustworthy as a result – then we benefit from the evidence that it is possible to have conflict and survive it together.

The dynamism of relational, transpersonal approaches

This book has been written in the service of pointing towards an evolving way of working with transpersonal approaches to create resilient, realistic and direct relationships that are exciting, illuminating and inspiring.

It is worthwhile developing an intention to trust ourselves as therapists and to see our clients' journeys as inextricably connected to our own, so that sessions are insightful and meaningful for both therapist and client, as we become more skilful at creating relationships that are blueprints for a more dynamic way of relating to the world in general.

If transpersonal approaches are to become increasingly significant in the therapeutic world then practitioners must not stay in ivory towers where transpersonal concepts are philosophically in the background, held as theoretical ways of thinking, without that theory becoming dynamically applicable in the here and now of the therapeutic encounter. We must take risks if we are to uncover and discover the truth within ourselves and our relationships with each other and the world.

My profound hope is that this book, in a small way, contributes to a way of working that is catalytic and in the service of living more effective and fulfilling lives, both in the consulting room and beyond it.

Bibliography

American Psychiatric Association. *Diagnostic and statistical manual of mental disorders (DSM-5®)*. Arlington, VA: American Psychiatric Publishing, 2013.

Assagioli, Roberto. *Psychosynthesis*. London: Thorsons, 1965.

Assagioli, Roberto. *Psychosynthesis: A Manual of Principles and Techniques*. London: Thorsons, 1993.

Davis, Madeleine, and David Wallbridge. *Boundaries and Space: An introduction to the work of D.W. Winnicott*. London: H. Karnac Books Ltd., 1981.

Ferrucci, Piero. *What We May Be: The Vision and Techniques of Psychosynthesis*. London: Mandala, 1990.

Firman, John, and Ann Gila. *The Primal Wound: A transpersonal view of trauma, addiction, and growth*. New York: State University of New York Press, 1997.

Frohlich, Herbert. 'Evidence for Bose condensation-like excitation of coherent modes in biological systems', *Physics Letters A* (Elsevier) 51, no. 1 (1975). pp. 21 – 22.

Goodbread, Joseph H. *Radical Intercourse: How dreams unite us in love, conflict and other inevitable relationships*. Portland, OR: Lao Tse Press, l997.

Hardy, Jean. *Psychology with a Soul*. London: Woodgrange Press, 1996,

Hardy, Jean. *There is Another World, but it is This One*. London: QUG, 1988.

Kuhn, Thomas. *The Structure of Scientific Revolutions*. 1962; Chicago, IL, and London: University of Chicago Press, 1970.

Kwok, M., Palmer, M. and Ramsey, J. (trans). *Tao Te Ching*. USA, Australia, Great Britain: Elements Books Ltd., 1993.

Mansfield, Victor, and J. Marvin Spiegelman. 'On the Physics and Psychology of the Transference as an Interactive Field', *Journal of Analytical Psychology* 41, no. 2 (1996). pp. 179 – 202.

Mindell, Amy, and Arnold Mindell. *Metaskills: The spiritual art of therapy.* Tempe, AZ: New Falcon Publications, 1993.

Mindell, Arnold. Coma: *The dreambody near death,* 2nd edn. London: Penguin Books Ltd., 1987.

O'Murchu, Diarmuid. *Quantum theology: Spiritual implications of the new physics.* Dublin: Gill and Macmillan Ltd., 1997.

Rosselli, Massimo, and Duccio Vanni, "Roberto Assagioli and Carl Gustav Jung", *The Journal of Transpersonal Psychology* 46 (2014. p. 8.

Schwartz-Salant, Nathan. *The Borderline Personality: Vision and healing.* Wilmette, IL: Chiron Publications, 1989.

Schwartz-Salant, Nathan, and Murray Stein, eds, *Transference and Countertransference.* Wilmette, IL: Chiron Publications, 1984.

Shultz, D., and S. Shultz. *Theories of Personality,* 9th edn. Belmont, CA: Wadsworth, Cengage Learning, 2009.

Whitmore, Diana. *Psychosynthesis Counselling in Action.* London: Sage Publications Ltd., 1991.

Zohar, Danah, and Ian N. Marshall, *The Quantum Self: Human nature and consciousness defined by the new physics.* New York: William Morrow and Company, Inc., 1990.

Index

Coming soon...

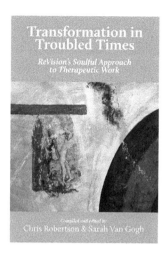

To celebrate its 30 years of pioneering work in the fields of counselling and psychotherapy training, the ReVision Centre for Transpersonal & Integrative Therapy has brought together a selection of writing by practitioners and teachers who have worked at the heart of the organization.

The chapters address a social and cultural crisis which, at this point in the history of our planet, needs new ways of looking at therapy and how it relates to the world beyond the consulting room. Just as 'the personal is political' was a way of seeing individual issues within the context of a wider political field, so we now need to see that the soul is a different kind of agency from that of the ego – one that is both internal and external, individual and cultural. The world may have lost connection with soul in its obsession with merchandise and control, but soul has not lost connection with us. These chapters offer an integrative perspective that both gives a place to the troubles of the modern world and also develops a well-tuned craft to firstly attend to our painful wounds and ultimately transform their bitterness into the salt of wisdom.

This book is a compelling work for psychotherapists, counsellors, trainees, and anyone interested in how psychotherapy influences and is influenced by the state of the planet, by imagination and by the reality of how politics impact on our daily lives.

ISBN 978-1-912-618-02-8 (print) / 978-1-912618-03-5 (ebook)

TransPersonal
Press

Lightning Source UK Ltd.
Milton Keynes UK
UKHW020204010919
348896UK00016B/1138/P